DITCHING FROM THE CLAYTON ROAD.

THE HISTORY OF DITCHLING

IN THE COUNTY OF SUSSEX.

BY

HENRY CHEAL, JUN.,

Organist of St. Margaret's Church, Ditchling.

———

Illustrated by Arthur B. Packham.

———

DEDICATED TO THE VICAR.

Santa Margareta

Amy Sawyer,
Artist, Ditchling.

Lewes :
LEWES & SOUTH COUNTIES PRESS LIMITED.

———

1901.

Facsimile of the first edition
published by Country Books ©2004
reprinted 2005, 2006, 2008, 2009, 2011

ISBN 978 1 898941 89 7

Country Books
Courtyard Cottage, Little Longstone, Bakewell, Derbyshire DE45 1NN
Tel: 01629 640670
e-mail: dickrichardson@country-books.co.uk
www.countrybooks.biz

Printed and bound in England by 4edge Ltd, Hockley, Essex.

PREFACE.

To one of antiquarian tastes it is always a source of great pleasure to trace the history of an ancient town or parish, more especially of a place which in the course of many years has—in outward appearance at least—but little altered, and preserves at the opening of the twentieth century some external evidence of its former importance, either in ancient buildings, memorials of the dead, or curious customs.

It is a pleasant task to relate some legend or folklore, to conjure up pictures of the past and to revive old time memories, to strive to people some ancient and half decayed mansion with its former inhabitants, to linger over the air of mystery which envelops such a place, to thrust aside as it were the veil between the present and past, though it is but a glimpse we may obtain, and that of "a faded tapestry," so faded indeed in places, that it is with difficulty and only after much diligent research we can read the subject and determine who and what are the characters thereon depicted.

To a casual visitor, Ditchling of to-day appears as an obscure Sussex village, situated in a romantic district which abounds in pretty scenery and delightful views, the joy of those who depict on canvas the beauties of nature and architecture, but a place which possesses little in common with larger places and modern towns.

This to a certain extent is true. The place no longer holds its position as a Sussex town; no longer does it bask in the sunshine of Royal favour and the prosperity attending it; no longer do Kings or Princes with long and gorgeous train of nobles and retainers in glittering cavalcade come hither to sojourn for a season to hunt in the forests or to hawk on the downs. Its ancient yearly fair, extending over three days, and its weekly markets are forgotten, and even its two minor fairs are but a memory, and the coaches which erstwhile were wont to rattle down its High Street are a thing of the past.

It must be evident to anyone who studies the matter at all that Ditchling has altered, not in outward appearance, but as a town, and from a business point of view, and it is probable that at the period when Brighton or Brighthelmstone is described as having been "a mere fishing village," this place ranked fairly high amongst the towns of Sussex. Let not the reader infer by this, however, that Ditchling has entirely lost its prosperity; on the contrary, we believe it is a very thriving little place, and even now we may describe its aspect as "Towny," for a considerable amount of business is carried on by the inhabitants.

The task which we have attempted has extended over a considerable period; we have referred to many works dealing with the general history and antiquities of the county, as well as to original and authentic documents from various sources.

The author begs to acknowledge with best thanks the kind assistance and many valuable suggestions so readily accorded him by Lieut.-Colonel F. W. T. Attree, R.E., F.S.A., and to the Rev. F. C. Norton, Vicar of Ditchling, whose antiquarian researches have added much to the interest of the work.

For the vignette of St. Margaret's head appearing on title page we are indebted to Miss Amy Sawyer.

The names of some of the earlier Rectors and Vicars of Ditchling are taken from the Chichester Clergy Lists, by the Rev. G. Hennessy.

CONTENTS.

	PAGE
Introduction	ix
CHAPTER I.	
Ancient Ditchling—The Manors	1
CHAPTER II.	
Ditchling Park	14
CHAPTER III.	
An Ancient Mansion and its Tenants	28
CHAPTER IV.	
Old Inhabitants	39
CHAPTER V.	
Miscellaneous Notes	47
CHAPTER VI.	
St. Margaret's Church	54
CHAPTER VII.	
Ecclesiastical Notes — Rectors and Vicars of Ditchling	71
CHAPTER VIII.	
Monumental Inscriptions and Memorials ...	90
CHAPTER IX.	
The Ditchling Meeting House	110
CHAPTER X.	
The "Jernel" of a Ditchling Man	122
CHAPTER XI.	
The Neighbourhood	133
Appendices	140
Index	167

LIST OF ILLUSTRATIONS.

	PAGE
Ditchling from the Clayton Road. Frontispiece.	
View from Pond Green	8
Entrance from Keymer	24
The Ancient House	30
An Old Corner	38
The Church from the Ancient House	56
Interior of the Church	64
Ditchling Vicarage in the year 1820	70
The Poole Monument	96
The Church in 1780	104
The Meeting House	112
The Cross, Plumpton	132

INTRODUCTION.

Ditchling, or Ditchelling, is situated in the county of Sussex, about eight miles north-west of Lewes, and eight north of Brighton, and a mile and a half east of Hassocks Station, on the London, Brighton, and South Coast main line. The parish is situated in the administrative county of East Sussex, Mid or Lewes Parliamentary Division, Lewes Union (until recently Chailey), Lewes Rape, Petty Sessional Division and County Court District, Rural Deanery of Lewes (Second Division), Archdeaconry of Lewes and Diocese of Chichester. The parish is included in the Hundred of Street, but was formerly in Swanborough, or, as the ancient spelling has it, "Soanberge."

The boundaries of the parish are as follows: North, Wivelsfield; south, Stanmer and Patcham; east, Westmeston; and west, Keymer. Its length is about seven miles, and its width rather more than a mile and a half on an average. The area is about 4,183 acres, a large portion of which is down and common land, including the highest point of the South Downs in East Sussex, Ditchling Beacon.

The soil of the northern part of the parish is a stiff clay, and contains beds of Sussex marble, the tract lying between the town and the chalk downs being composed of a rich calcareous loam on clay. The principal crops grown are wheat, hay, beans, peas, and turnips, and hops were formerly grown at Court Gardens in this parish, but have not been cultivated for many years.

Blackbrook, which is a considerable stream, rises between Ditchling and Street, and gives name to a farm. Flowing eastward to Hurst Barn, it joins not far from that spot a fine stream which rises in the moat of the old mansion of Plumpton Place and drives several water-mills. These united waters flow under Bevan and Barcombe Bridges, and so to the Ouse.

A small rivulet known as the Pods Stream rises on Ditchling Common, and flows westward to St. John's Common and Wyndham Bridge, where it joins a tributary of the Adur.

A chalybeate spring on Ditchling Common was formerly much resorted to for its medicinal virtues, but its exact locality is now hardly known.

The town, which is situated on a gentle acclivity of reddish sandstone, stands at the junction of the main roads from Lewes to Henfield, and Brighton to East Grinstead, and is cruciform in arrangement; it is lighted by gas supplied by the Keymer and Ditchling Gas Company from their works at Hassocks, established 1867, and the water supply is from the Burgess Hill Water Company's works, which are situated in a combe on the northern slopes of the downs in this parish. The quality of the water has been declared by experts to be exceptionally pure. The numerous disused grassy lanes so noticeable in the parish are the old " Whapple Ways," " a way where a cart and horses cannot pass, but horses only ' (Sussex). Their direction may be easily traced.

The principal landowners are the Marquis of Abergavenny, K.G. (Lord of the Manor of Ditchling); Mentor Mott, Esq.; J. E. Hunt, Esq.; Mrs. Crofton, of London; Miss J. Tanner, of Patcham; the Earl of Chichester; Sampson Copestake, Esq., of Shermanbury Park, Henfield; and the owners of St. George's Retreat. Of the Manors, of which there are several besides the principal, we shall treat later. The rateable value of the parish is £8,473.

The population in 1801 was 706; in 1811, 740;

1821, 844; 1831, 917; 1841, 1,148; 1851, 1,082; 1861, 1,061; 1871, 1,271; 1881, 1,342; 1891, 1,226.

We believe the brick-making industry is in a great measure responsible for the fluctuation in numbers. The clay has long been worked on the Common, where there is an old established terra-cotta and brick manufactory. The majority of the inhabitants are engaged in agricultural pursuits.

In the year 1801 there are said to have been only 93 houses in Ditchling parish, which had, however, increased in 1821 to 124. Now (1899) there are considerably more than 200.

The National Schools, which were erected about 1844, and enlarged in 1887, form a picturesque group of buildings overlooking the pond.

There is a Convalescent Home in connection with the Sussex County Hospital, and also some cottage homes for lightermen and watermen of the River Thames, the latter erected by the late William Vokins, Esq., in 1888.

On Ditchling Common is a Roman Catholic institution for the insane, St. George's Retreat, which was founded by the late Very Rev. Canon Maes, and erected in 1870. The buildings stand in well-kept grounds, which cover 280 acres, the institution being under the management of the Sisters of St. Augustine. The chapel services are open to the public.

The Baptists have a small chapel in the parish.

THE HISTORY OF DITCHLING.

CHAPTER I.

Ancient Ditchling. The Manors.

The history of Ditchling may safely be said to date from Saxon times, but it will be well before examining this period, to note the traces which are left of even earlier inhabitants than our Saxon forefathers.

Firstly, there are evidences of those early inhabitants of Britain whose weapons of warfare were fashioned out of flint, and you cannot walk even a very short distance on the adjacent downs without finding an abundance of the fragments of these weapons scattered broadcast over the land.

Secondly, the discovery—many years ago now—of several weighty masses of molten copper and a bronze celt at a spot not far from the chalybeate spring on Ditchling Common suggested the very probable idea that there had been a manufactory there in ancient times.

Thirdly, in more recent years a Roman fibula was ploughed up in a field in the parish. This article, which is not unlike a pair of tweezers, was an instrument used for drawing the flesh together after a wound.

Ditchling Beacon was undoubtedly a stronghold of the Romans, who have left evidence of their occupation in the camp, which is on the Beacon, the earthworks being distinctly Roman in character.

From time to time Roman coins have been discovered at or near this spot, and among others may be mentioned one of Tiberius, who was second Emperor of Rome, and reigned A.D. 14 to 37. This coin had on the obverse side the head of the Emperor laureated " T. Caesar Aug F. Augustus," and on the reverse, a woman sitting holding a lance and a branch of laurel, also the words " Pontiff Maxim." And in those ancient and far distant times the scene from the summit of this noble hill was a very different one from what it is to-day.

No smiling landscape with its countless homesteads, pastures, mansions, and parks was at that time spread like a garden over the weald of Sussex, but a trackless forest covering the whole of the district, a forest whose gloomy depths had as yet scarce been trod by the foot of man, a dense dark jungle, infested with beasts of prey and countless other dangers, its very name signifying an unfrequented and untrodden spot. It was the great forest of Andred or Anderida.

But passing on to Saxon times—and here we find more reliable history—Ditchling was a Royal Manor, one of those several Sussex Manors owned by King Alfred the Great, with whom the history and traditions of the place are closely associated.

This monarch spent much time in Sussex, and we may mention that (according to Asser) his father, Ethelwulf, was buried in the church of Steyning, a neighbouring parish.

The origin of the name Ditchling appears to be Saxon. Let us examine its derivation and meaning.

It has been variously spelt at different periods thus: Diccelingum, Dicelinges, Dicheningh, Dykeninge, Dyceling, Diceling, Dicelinge, Ditchelling, and at the present day Ditchling.

Now, as Dice or Dike is the Saxon word for a fence, which, however, need not be formed of wood, but may be composed of earth or stone, or thrown up by entrenchment (as at the Devil's Dyke), and as the Anglo-Saxon word Dykening signifies an enclosure, the generally accepted theory has been that the whole or greater part of the land in the Parish of Ditchling was enclosed at a very early date in English history. It may have been, and probably was, by means of a rough wall formed of masses of chalk and rubble, such a wall as later years encompassed the town of Lewes.

We may also quote the following on the origin of the word Ditchling by the Rev. Edmund McLure, M.A., M.R.I.A., F.L.S.: "The best text of King Alfred's Will (XI. Century) quotes Diccelingum, i.e., the dative or locative plural of Diccelingas. Domesday (as we shall presently note) gives Dicelinges. The Taxation of Pope Nicholas (1291) gives Dicheningh with the variation Digmerg and Wyvelesfeld. Digmerg seems to be for Dic mearce, Dyke boundary. Place words ending in 'ingas' are numerous, such as Paccingas (Patching), Angemeringas (Angmering), etc. Generally 'ing' means 'belonging to,' but in North English names is often a different word and means meadow."

"As the earliest recorded forms of the word Ditchling are Diccelingum and Dicelingas, i.e., Diccel and Dicel, *not* Diccheninge or Dykeninge, i.e., Dice or Dyke, one must obviously look for a form containing 'l.' It has recently been suggested that Dicul, who was Abbot of Bosham, and was a Lindisfarne (Scotie) missioner at Selsey when St. Wilfrid arrived there, gave his name to Ditchling, and so it became Diculingas, 'belonging to Dicul,' or 'Dicul's meadows.'"

As King Alfred the Great owned the Manor of Ditchling, doubtless he it was who formed the park, and it seems not unlikely that in the latter years of his reign, and when he had freed his country somewhat from the invasion of the Danes, he sometimes resorted here for the purpose of hunting or hawking, for of these sports history tells us he was very fond.

At his death, the Manor of Ditchling passed to his kinsman Osferth, to whom he had willed it. The will is preserved in the British Museum to this day. Thus the first mention of Ditchling in written records now extant, dates back to 1,000 years, for we note the year 1901 completes ten centuries since the death of one of the greatest and wisest of England's many monarchs.

Of Osferth we know little, except that he owned the Manor, but for how long a period we cannot tell, the next owner mentioned being Edward the Confessor.

Whether this monarch ever visited Ditchling is uncertain, but very probable, as he owned other manors in Sussex.

It was not long after his death that William, Duke of Normandy laid claim to the Saxon crown on a pretence that it had been promised him by Edward, and finding his claim resisted, invaded the country, and fought the decisive battle of Hastings (1066), wresting the crown from the brave King Harold, and the country from its rightful owner.

To the most powerful of his followers he gave large tracts of the beautiful country which he had invaded. Ditchling, amongst other enormous possessions, he lavished on William de Warenne, the husband of either his daughter or sister Gundrada.

In 1086 the Domesday Book was compiled, and in this wonderful volume appears the following description:—

" In Soanberge Hundred," viz., Swanborough.

" William himself (i.e., de Warenne) holds Dicelinges, King Edward held it. It has never paid geld (land tax). In the time of King Edward it vouched for 46 hides. When received only 42 hides, the others were in the rape of the Earl of Mortaine, and 6 woods which belonged to the head of the manor. It now vouches for 33 hides. There is land for 60 ploughs. In demesne are 8 ploughs; and 108 villeins and 40 bordars have 80 ploughs and one. There is a church and a mill of 30 pence and 130 acres of meadow. Wood for 80 hogs. In Lewes 11 masures of twelve shillings.

"Of this land Gilbert holds 1 hide and a half, Hugh 2 hides, Alward 3 hides, Warin 3 hides, Richard 1 hide. In demesne they have 7 ploughs and a half with 29 bordars, and 3 villeins and 10 serfs with 3 ploughs. In Lewes 6 burgesses of 43 pence.

"The whole Manor in the time of King Edward was worth £80 and 66d. and afterwards £25. Now William's demesne £60 and his men's £10 and 10 shillings."

Other information runs as follows:—

"The Earl (Mortaine) himself holds Ferlega for one rod. It is outside the Rape, in the Rape of Lewes. It lay at Dicelinges. It has never paid geld. There is land for half a plough. There is one villein with 1 plough. It was worth 10 shillings now 5 shillings."

"Ansfrid holds 2 hides, less one rod, outside the Rape of the Earl. King Edward held them. They lay in the Manor of Diceninges, and have not paid geld. There is land for 6 ploughs wood and herbage for 6 hogs. There is 1 acre of meadow and one smithy. There are 6 villeins with 2 ploughs. In the time of King Edward they were worth 15 shillings. Now 20 shillings."

NOTE.—"*Villeins*" were persons in absolute servitude who, with their children and effects, belonged to the lord of the soil like the cattle and stock on it. "*Bordars*" may be translated cottagers; a "*masure*" signifies a house and land in a borough.

"*Serfs*" seem to have been a lower order of villeins, and possibly performed more servile work.

The church mentioned in the Domesday Survey is believed to have been built by Alfred the Great, and some authorities tell us that it is incorporated in, and forms part of, the present building; but be that as it may, there seems to be little doubt that it occupied the same site. The water-mill, whose owner was William de Warenne, and the rental of which was 30 pence per annum, has entirely disappeared, the very spot forgotten, and all trace of it lost in the mists of antiquity.

The early history of Ditchling is in a great measure a history of the proud Earls de Warenne, who also held the Earldom of Surrey. Their stronghold was Lewes Castle. As Lords of the Manor of Ditchling (which descended like the barony of Lewes), we find frequent reference to them in many old deeds. They held possession for three and a half centuries, and then the Manor passed to the Fitz-Alans, Earls of Arundel, who were heirs general, and afterwards, on the division of the estates after the death of Thomas Fitz-Alan, fifth Earl of Arundel, to the Nevilles, who still hold it.

The Manor of Ditchling extends a considerable distance beyond the borders of the parish, and embraces parts of the parishes of Chailey, Ardingly, Balcombe, and Worth. The Manor Rolls begin in 1597. Westwick is a copyhold held of Ditchling Manor, and is thus described in the Court Rolls:

"All that customary tenement, and two large lands called Westwick, with pasture for four oxen yearly, to be fed in Ditchling Park, from the feast called Hoptide until the feast of St. Andrew the Apostle (November 30th) to the same tenement and lands belonging."

Hoptide here mentioned is believed to mean "Hock Tide," which was an ancient festival constantly observed in England to celebrate the day on which the English had obtained a great victory over the Danes. It occurred every year on the Tuesday fortnight after Easter week, and was known as "Hock Tuesday," when it was the custom of the landlord to give his tenants, who were really his servants, leave to celebrate the day, and they in turn paid him a duty which was called "Hock Money."

There are four minor manors in this parish, Ditchling Rectory, or Dimocks, Ditchling Garden, Camois Court, and Pellingworth, or Pedlingworth.

Ditchling Rectory or Dimocks extends into the

VIEW FROM POND GREEN.

parishes of Ditchling and Patcham. The Manor Rolls begin in 1650.

In the 27th year of the reign of Henry VIII., the Prior of St. Pancras, by indenture, demised the Lordship of the Manor of Ditchling Rectory to John More for 40 years, at the rent of £6 6s. 8d. per year. In the 13th year of Elizabeth's reign, the Queen granted the reversion to the Dean and Chapter of Chichester, and the Lord of the Manor since that date has been the Chancellor of Chichester Cathedral. From the Valor Ecclesiasticus of 1535 we learn that John More was also at this date farmer of the Rectory of Ditchling, with all the profits and with the chapel of Wyvesfeld, valued at £10 per annum; he was then head of the family of More, of Morehouse, in Wivelsfield. The descent of the impropriate Rectory of Ditchling will be given in Chapter VII.

In 1547, Richard Adeane, alias Warren, by his will proved at Lewes in 1550, left his Manor of Dymocks, in Ditchling, to his son Henry, who by his will, proved in 1571, left his wife lands called Democke for life, after whose death the Manor probably became the property of the Dean and Chapter of Chichester.

"The fines of the copyholders are arbitrary. Cottages pay 6d. for a fine certain. All the half-yard lands holden of this manor are on the east side of the highway from the downs to Ditchling Common and eight sheep leases on Ditchling Downs. The manor is belonging to and part of the aforesaid impropriate rectory of Ditchling and the lands held of it by copy are called 'The Glebe Lands' thereof, and in the leases made of the Rectory by the Chancellor (of Chichester Cathedral) the said Manor hath been from time to time excepted, and is taken to be excepted in the last lease made of the rectory, and so to be in present possession as aforesaid" (Burrell MS.).

Ditchling Garden Manor Rolls begin in 1622. This Manor formed part of the lands belonging to the Priory of St. Pancras, at Southover (Lewes), and in the Valor Ecclesiasticus of 1535 is returned as in the hands of the Prior for the use of his house, and containing 80 acres of pasture and 30 acres of meadow, of the annual value of £6.

The rents of the Manor in the parishes of Dychenyng, Twynam, Bolney, Slaugham, Chiltington, and Hurst are given as amounting to £13 5s. 11d., and the perquisites of the Court there in ordinary years are estimated at 10s. As deductions, the rent resolute to the Lords of the Barony of Lewes is stated to be 6d. per annum, and the annual fee to William Rygge, the bailiff or steward of the Manor, 30s. 4d.

The Priory of St. Pancras, before mentioned, was founded about the year 1078 by William de Warenne and his wife, the Countess Gundrada, and completed by their son. Its monks, of the Cluniac order, were a branch of the Benedictines, and St. Pancras was the first house of that denomination in England. The endowments of this place are said to have been enormous, its Prior was mitred and a peer of the realm, and there were very few, if any, monasteries in England which enjoyed so wide a reputation. The first Prior, Lanzo, is stated to have been a man of great piety and learning.

Amongst those noble families who added to its endowments and found sepulture in its church were the De Warennes, Clares, De Veres, St. Johns, Fitz-Alans, De Lancasters, and Nevilles. The great church, which in size and beauty of architecture was equal to most cathedrals, together with its chapter house, cloisters, and other buildings, made up an enormous and noble group which occupied, with its gardens, an area of forty acres.

To this Priory William, second Earl De Warenne, granted by deed his Manor of the "Garden of Dychening, with a wood and lands and free pasture for cattle in the pastures of Dychening and Chiemere."

THE HISTORY OF DITCHLING.

From the Register of Lewes Priory, we learn that Alfrey de Falmer sold to John Todeherste a moiety of his mill, on the lands of the monks of Lewes at Ditchling, for 8 marks and five shillings. The witnesses are Hugh de Plumpton, Phillip de Rottingdean, Alexander de Ditchling, Alexander, son of Sade, etc. The deed is undated.

At the dissolution of the religious houses by Henry VIII., in 1537, the revenues were estimated at a sum equal to £10,000 at the present day, revenues which the King, after demolishing the beautiful church and other buildings, appropriated to his own use or gave to whom he would; and how effectually the work of destruction was carried out, a few scattered fragments of the once noble pile bear silent witness.

Little wonder was it that the Priory of St. Pancras had flourished. Enjoying the protection of the mighty Earls De Warenne, and being but a short distance from their stronghold, Lewes Castle, they had for centuries defied their enemies, and all who sought to do them hurt; but in the time of Henry things were different, the power of the Barons had long since been broken by the Wars of the Roses, and the De Warennes had passed away for ever.

After the dissolution, Henry granted Ditchling Garden and Rectory Manors, with the other possessions of St. Pancras Priory, to Thomas, Lord Cromwell, and on Cromwell's attainder in 1540 to Anne of Cleves, his repudiated wife. The following is an extract from the artfully worded deed which conveyed them to that Princess:—

"Willing to yield to the laws of the realm, to discharge even her own conscience from this pretended marriage, to enjoy her own liberty and to remain in our kingdom," Henry granted to her "manors and lands and tenements for the sustentation maintenance and augmentation of the noble rank of Lady Anne of Cleves," amongst which was included "the Manor of

Ditchling, with all and every of its members and appurtenances besides all those our rectories of Dychening (and others) lately belonging or appertaining to the Monastery of Lewes or Parsels of the same monastery and the rents of assize to our said Rectory of Ditchling in our said County of Sussex."

As we are now only dealing with the Manors, we will not in this place treat further of the connection of Anne of Cleves with Ditchling, but will refer to her in the succeeding pages.

In the 19th year of Elizabeth's reign, Ditchling Garden Manor is stated to have comprised 20 messuages, 4 cottages, 20 barns, 200 acres arable land, 50 acres pasture, 100 acres heath and furze, 100 acres meadow, 200 acres wood. In the second year of Elizabeth's reign, Thomas Beard senr. and junr., mortgaged the Manor for £300, in 1570 John Gomayin (?) was Lord of the Manor, in 1615 Mr. Nye, in 1679 Thomas Gage, Gent., in 1687 Thomas Beard, Esquire, in 1702 Thomas Midmer, Gentleman, in 1727 Thomas Geere, in 1762 Dr. Russell, in 1763 W. Kempe, in 1816 James Ingram, Esquire.

We believe we are correct in stating that Dr. Russell here mentioned was the founder of Brighton, and W. Kempe, his son, who practised as a barrister and took his mother's maiden name, was long known as Sergeant Kempe of Malling, where he resided. We shall note that the Manor of Pellingworth was also in the possession of Sergeant Kempe.

Camois Court Manor embraces parts of the parishes of Ditchling, Barcombe, and Newick. The Manor Rolls begin in 1662. In the 15th year of Elizabeth it was owned by William Morgan and Anthony Stapley, and in 1674 William Lane, of Southover (ancestor of H. C. Lane, Esq., of Middleton), on the marriage of his daughter Elizabeth with John Smith, of Hamsey, granted to them and their heirs the moiety of this lordship, of which he was himself possessed. At the beginning of Queen Anne's reign, Thomas Medley, of Coneyburrows, purchased of the Smiths their moiety, and at this time the Lucas family were proprietors of the other moiety. In 1826, Lucas Shadwell, Esquire, was Lord.

Pellingworth or Pedlingworth, the smallest of the Ditchling Manors, is in Stanmer Park, and was formerly in the possession of Mr. Sergeant Kempe. In 1788 and 1790 Anne and Lucy Lucas qualified a gamekeeper for this Manor.

In our researches into the ancient history of Ditchling we have met with frequent references to many Sussex families of note, directly or indirectly connected with this place. One of these is the family of Borde.

"George Neville Lord Abergavenny by deed dated 27th June 2 Henry VIII. enfranchised Andrew Borde, son of John Borde, his native or villein belonging to his Manor of Dycheling and made him free from all bondage, villainage and servile condition so that neither the said Lord nor his heirs nor anyone else on their account should for the time to come have any right or claim upon the said Andrew nor on his goods or chattels."

It is probable that the father of the above-mentioned Andrew Borde was an inhabitant of Cuckfield, where, soon after, the family began to rise into opulence and importance. They built Board Hill in Cuckfield, and Paxhill, Lindfield, and a branch of the family settled at each place. Of this family was the far-famed Andrew Borde, the physician and humorist of Pevensey.

CHAPTER II.

DITCHLING PARK.

As our notes on this subject are very closely interwoven with the history of the De Warenne family, a few necessary facts concerning them and some further notes on their connection with the principal Manor will now be given.

The Earls of Surrey and Lords of Lewes were proud, haughty, and powerful, and no less than eight in succession exercised their feudal rights in Sussex and enjoyed, with occasional terms of confiscation, the enormous possessions which William the Conqueror had bestowed on their ancestor.

But of all his race, John de Warenne, seventh Earl of Surrey, and Lord of Lewes from 1240 till 1304, seems to have been the most arbitrary and over-bearing.

Probably the most powerful noble of his time, he was, like most of his ancestors, closely associated with, and allied to, the Royal Family, having married Alicia, half sister of Henry III.

A close adherent of King Henry throughout that troublous period, so eloquently described in that splendid work, "The Baron's War" (Blaauw), John de Warenne, having put his Castle of Lewes in a state of defence, and mustered his forces, received the King in that town a few days before the memorable battle ; and the Royal army encamped without the town, the monarch being entertained with great ceremony at the Priory of Southover.

With the King came his brother Richard, King of the Romans, and the gallant, but impetuous Prince Edward, who found entertainment at the Castle.

THE HISTORY OF DITCHLING.

Meanwhile, a considerable army had flocked to the banner set up by Simon de Montfort, and marching into Sussex, reached Fletching Common and encamped there, and two Bishops were sent to Lewes by de Montfort, in order to negotiate, if it were possible, terms of peace with the King.

These prelates were unsuccessful in their errand; the King received them in state, surrounded by many of his most powerful nobles, but rejected de Montfort's terms in the most decided manner.

De Montfort now decided to give battle to the Royalist army, and accordingly before break of day on the 14th of May, 1264, he led his forces towards Lewes, and having mustered them, on the downs, two or three miles north-west of the town, addressed them, promising them if they should fall in the battle a quick entry into heaven.

Meanwhile, news of their approach had reached the King, who, dividing his soldiers into three bodies, himself leading one, and Prince Edward and Richard, King of the Romans, the other two, advanced to the attack, accompanied by many powerful nobles (among whom, of course, was John de Warenne), followed by their retainers.

Then began one of the most deadly conflicts, yet one of the most important battles, ever decided on English soil.

Among those who had flocked to de Montfort's standard, were numbered a considerable following of Londoners, who were for the most part undisciplined.

They were commanded by Lord Seagrave.

On these Prince Edward opened the battle with a furious onslaught, against which they were utterly unable to stand. Giving way in all directions, they fled across the downs, hotly pursued by the Prince and his soldiers, who, with relentless fury, cut them to pieces. Hundreds fled down the steep sides of the downs, and were intercepted and slaughtered in the valleys below;

hundreds more fled westward towards Plumpton Plain, in which direction numerous traces of the terrible battle have from time to time been discovered in bones and weapons.

The fury of the Prince seems to have been excited by the remembrance of an insult which had been offered to the Queen, his mother, some time previously by the populace of London.

The Queen, it would seem, intending to journey to Windsor by water, had set out from the Tower in the Royal barge, but the citizens assembled on London Bridge had thrown refuse and stones at it, and it is stated would have tried to sink it when passing under the bridge, had it not been for the interference of the Lord Mayor.

This indignity the gallant and impetuous Prince Edward had not forgotten, and he exacted a terrible revenge at Lewes. So eager was he in pursuing the luckless Londoners, that it was late in the afternoon when he returned to the scene of the battle, and then only to find that his own recklessness in leaving the field had contributed in no small degree to the utter defeat of the Royal army, and his father and uncle, with many others of his friends, made prisoners.

The important results of the battle of Lewes—in which it is said no less a number, and possibly more than 5,000 Englishmen were slaughtered by their own countrymen—are well known, and the "Mise of Lewes," which was drawn up on the following day, may justly be considered as one of the foundations of English Law and Liberty.

In the meanwhile, John de Warenne, seeing that the cause of the King was lost, deserted him in his hour of need, and in the evening of the day of battle, under cover of nightfall, when we are told the streets of Lewes ran with blood and were filled with the bodies of the slaughtered, escaped from the town in company with several companions, and reaching the coast, afterwards found a refuge on the Continent.

For a time he lost all his estates, recovering them only after the battle of Evesham, in 1265, when the Royal party retrieved the disaster sustained at Lewes.

John de Warenne, we are told, exercised his feudal rights in Sussex in a most arbitrary manner, and for the sake of preserving his hares and wild game, fined at will and imprisoned in his Castle at Lewes all who hunted; his warrens became so full and over-run with game that they destroyed nearly all the corn grown near them, which, however, he would not allow the farmers to protect, either by hedge or fence, on pain of imprisonment. He encroached upon the King's highway in many places in Sussex, and enclosed the town of Lewes with a stone wall without warrant.

His park at Ditchling was watched and guarded most strictly, and no one was allowed to pass through it without serious consequences ensuing. Several cases of assault are mentioned in connection with this arbitrary conduct, and the following incident, which took place in the reign of Edward I., is recorded in the Hundred Rolls, Vol. ii., p 213 :—

Matthew de Hastings, Sheriff of Surrey and Sussex, paid an official visit to the neighbourhood of Ditchling in 1272, and it is reported that when he came below Hayle (Hayley in Westmeston) there met him on the King's highway John de Niwent, Master of the Foresters of Clers, and Walter de Haldeleye, Master of the Foresters of Waldon, who arrested the progress of himself and his men, and forcibly took their arms from them, and carrying them off, retained them. After this, when the Sheriff sent his horse to Dichening to be shod, Walter Parker, of Dichening, accompanied by other men of the parish, beat and wounded the boy riding upon it, and robbed him. And as the Sheriff proceeded onwards, and had arrived at Pokehole, John

THE HISTORY OF DITCHLING.

Bacun, with his own men and the Foresters of the Earl of Warenne, met him in the King's highway, and again arresting his progress, violently forced from his custody Amicia, the wife of William Hocote, and carried her, together with the horse on which the Sheriff rode, to the house of Master John de Ferryng, at Chiltington; at whose instigation, and that of Alexander de Shyre, the assault is declared to have been perpetrated. Several other cases of assault are mentioned in connection with the visits of the Sheriff to the neighbourhood.

To answer these and many other charges, the Earl was at last summoned to appear before John de Reygate and other justices at Guildford, in 1279, on which occasion he was asked to produce his title deeds, and in answer to this drew forth his sword from its scabbard and exhibited that as his best title deed, "refusing not to answer the charges imputed to him, avowing that all he did belonged to his feudal rights, and that neither he nor his ancestors had ever encroached upon or usurped the King's rights," and furthermore, we are told, "the Earl was honourably dismissed from all suit."

From several circumstances we are led to infer that the Earl spent much of his time at Ditchling, for we know that he kept up a large stud of horses in the park there.

After his death, which occurred September 27th, 1304, the stud was purchased by Edward I. for his son, the first Prince of Wales, afterwards the ill-fated Edward II. Now the connection of Prince Edward with Ditchling came about in a very interesting manner.

He was at the time a young man of twenty-two, and had as his companion a certain Piers Gaveston, afterwards the notorious favourite who had been brought up at Court, and spent the greater part of his boyhood as the companion of the young Prince, but alas, as youth ripened into manhood, we find him, though described as a young man "conspicuous in person, courage, and wit," leading the Prince into a life of vice and profligacy, which ultimately brought them both into disgrace. Prince Edward's manner of living is thus quaintly described by an old chronicler:—

"Not caring to associate with the noble, he clave to buffoons, singers, actors, grooms, labourers, rowers, sailors, and mechanics, indulging in drinks, readily betraying secrets, striking by-standers on light occasion, etc."

This mode of life reached its climax when a special act of folly and riot took place. This was the breaking into the park of the Bishop of Chester, and killing his deer, in those days considered one of the greatest crimes of which anyone could be guilty; moreover, the Bishop was the King's Treasurer.

The punishment inflicted on the Prince was banishment, and he was forbidden to approach the Court for a period of many months, his friends were all dismissed, and amongst them, of course, Gaveston.

The period of his banishment Prince Edward passed in Sussex and Kent, and it was about this time that the stud of the Earl de Warenne at Ditchling was purchased for his use.

The Prince wrote many letters during his banishment and period of disgrace. One negotiating for the purchase of the stud runs as follows:—

"Inasmuch as our people have already spoken to you on our behalf that we wished to have the stud which belonged to the said Earl for the value, as it shall be appraised by honest persons, we again entreat, that the said stud may be kept for us wherever the Earl had it, and fix a time sure and convenient when our people and your people may examine the said stud and fix both a certain price and day to make the payment."

Another letter relating to this matter shows that it was successfully accomplished, and the Prince continued to keep his stud at Ditchling, while another epistle relating to the same subject, and written from Battle 28th day of June 1305, informs us that:—

"Brothers John de Burne and Sir Oliver de Wisset, executors of the Lord Earl de Warenne, are entreated for the love of the Prince to give assistance more speedily to John de Dychenynge, Keeper of the King's Colts, in those matters in which the said lord was bound to him concerning the time in which he served him. Given a la Battaille."

In plain English, to pay his wages.

No doubt "Keeper of the King's Colts" was an office of some importance.

A year or two after the purchase above recorded, the old King died (1307) and Prince Edward succeeded to the throne, and well for him would it have been if he had but learned the lesson of his banishment. We all know how he again took Piers Gaveston into favour, heaping abundance of riches and honour upon him, so that he became the most powerful noble in the kingdom, till at last the Barons became jealous of the honours conferred upon him, and finally compassed his downfall and death.

Surely this should have taught Edward II. that for a King to have favourites was bad policy; not so, he took others as worthless as Gaveston, and his rule becoming weaker and weaker, his enemies deposed and imprisoned him, until at last he suffered a horrible and cruel death in the gloomy dungeon in the keep of Berkeley Castle. He was buried in Gloucester Cathedral.

It is believed that this unfortunate King spent portions of his leisure at Ditchling, and took a considerable interest in the town and its welfare. In 1312, he granted to John de Warenne the right to hold a weekly market in Ditchling, on Tuesdays, and also a fair which was to last three days, viz., the eve, the day, and the morrow of the Feast of St. Margaret, July 19th, 20th, 21st. This John de Warenne was grandson of the

THE HISTORY OF DITCHLING.

seventh Earl, at whose death he had succeeded, his father having been killed at a tournament.

The mention of these markets and fairs will alone be sufficient to conjure up in our minds scenes of life and animation, quite unknown to the streets of Ditchling to-day, for on these occasions it presented a busy scene, and became a mart for all the country side.

The weekly market has long since been discontinued, and the three days' fair forgotten, indeed, it is thought that the two annual fairs which were held at Ditchling until within recent years were established to replace that event; one was held on April 5th, for sheep and hogs, and the other October 12th, for pedlary, but even these events have sunk into oblivion.

Returning to our notes on the park, it is recorded that in the year 1379, Richard, 4th Earl of Arundel and Surrey, to whom the Manor of Ditchling had descended on the death of his uncle, John, eighth Earl de Warenne, and the last of that mighty family, prosecuted a gang of 42 poachers, who, led by the parish priest of Rype, had made a raid on the Earl's free chase and warren at Cokefield, Dychenyng, Clayton, Pyecombe, Hurstpierpoint, etc., and carried off his hares, rabbits, and pheasants, and committed other depredations. The case, it seems, was tried in the King's Bench, but the sentence pronounced against these poachers we have not been able to discover; we may, however, be satisfied that it would be a very severe one, and probably death, if not to all, at least to the ringleaders of the gang.

Only two of the Fitz-Alans, viz., the fourth and fifth Earls of Arundel, held the Manor of Ditchling, for on the death of Thomas Fitz-Alan, fifth Earl, in 1415, it passed into the possession of the Nevilles, Lords Bergavenny, in which family it remains at the present day, in the person of the Marquis of Abergavenny.

The Countess of Arundel, widow of the late Earl, possessed for her lifetime the "Manor of Ditchling, with the park, called Ditchling Park, containing by estimation 300 acres, together with the Chase called Fritebergh and Shortfrith, containing together by estimation 500 acres."

This custom still continues with the Manor of Ditchling, viz., that the widow of the Lord holds it for her lifetime, or widowhood, as the case may be. It is interesting to notice that a monument to the above-named Thomas Fitz-Alan and his Countess Beatrix stands in the Sepulchral Chapel at Arundel. It is made of alabaster, and the Countess is represented wearing a peculiar horned head-dress.

The first member of the Neville family who held possession of Ditchling Manor, was Edward, Lord Bergavenny, who died in 1476; he also held, besides other parts of the Fitz-Alan estates, the Chase of Cleres and Forest of Worth.

There is little doubt that at this time the park at Ditchling was enclosed, for this is plainly stated by a demise which this Lord Edward and Sir Henry Neville made of the house and lands, within the pale of "Ditcheling Park," to William Overy, for the lives of himself and his sons, George, Robert, and Francis, at a rent of twenty pounds per annum.

While on the subject of the park, it is interesting to note the following facts in connection therewith. In Rowe's manuscript account of the different manorial customs of Sussex, occurs the following entry:—

"Lord Bergavenny's, 14th February, 39th Elizabeth, Ditcheling Park with house, buildings, land, meadows, etc., now enclosed within the pales, limits, or enclosures of the said Park."

In another entry Frankbarrough is called a free chase, and is identical with that referred to under the name of the Chase of Friteberg, and the Frankbarrow or Frankbar of the present day. The Chase of Cleres is not at this day to be identified, but was probably in the neighbourhood.

ENTRANCE FROM KEYMER.

Now, at the time Rowe's MS. was written, there must have been in existence a noteworthy house, and one which remains to this day. We allude, of course, to the picturesque structure standing opposite the entrance to the churchyard, which we will describe further.

Of another ancient mansion the foundations were discovered in 1846. It seems strange that all tradition of such a mansion having existed, and all trace of its position should have been lost, but so it was, until its extensive foundations were suddenly discovered. The site was in a field, on the east side of the Lodge Farm House, Keymer, forming part of a farm known as Park Farm, and though quite close to the parish boundaries of Keymer and Ditchling, and a small portion of the farm is in the former parish, yet the site of the ancient mansion is well within the Ditchling boundaries. There is no doubt that this mansion was the ancient hunting lodge within the Park of Ditchling, and probably Lodge Farm originally derived its name from its proximity to it before all traces had become obliterated. The story of the discovery is not without interest.

For many years a particular spot in the field had not been cultivated, owing to the fact that whenever an attempt was made to plough it, the resistance which it offered was such as to defy all efforts to cut through it.

At last the tenants of the farm determined to clear away the obstruction, whatever it was, and render the spot fit for cultivation, and in the course of this work the foundations of an ancient building were laid bare, an event which caused considerable excitement amongst the Sussex archæologists of that day. The walls were very substantial, being composed of flint, with an outer casing of stone, the whole being of great thickness; it was while clearing away the earth which had accumulated round these walls that at about the depth of three feet from the surface many fragments of ancient decorated paving tiles, and amongst them two almost perfect specimens, were found. These interesting tiles were impressed with heads in two different kinds of warlike costume, the outlines being remarkably distinct and sharp, although considerably worn. It was at first supposed that they were of Romano-British origin, but experts on such matters having carefully studied these specimens, came to the conclusion that they were of French manufacture; tiles of the same kind having been made at Neufchatel, in Normandy, about the time of Francis I., not earlier than 1530, or later than 1550.

It would be useless to speculate as to how or when what must once have been a mansion of considerable extent, fell into ruin, though we would fain know more of its history. Probably when once deserted it shared the fate of so many noble buildings in bygone days, and became a quarry for other buildings. That some of its materials were so used the following evidence will show.

Some time after the discovery of these ruins, the old church at Hurst was demolished, and while the excavations were being made for the foundations of the present church, some tiles of similar pattern were discovered, built into the walls of a very roughly-made vault, and as they were much worn by walking upon, the conclusion arrived at was that they originally were brought from the ruin at Ditchling. Unfortunately, however, owing to some misunderstanding, the workmen demolished the vault before further investigation could be made of the occurrence, or probably much more light might have been thrown on a very interesting subject.

There is yet another discovery in connection with these paving tiles, and this was in building the south aisle of Keymer Church, some more being turned up during the excavations for the walls.

While on the subject of discovery, another one of

THE HISTORY OF DITCHLING.

more recent years may be mentioned, especially as it seems to have a bearing on the subject of the park which we are considering.

This was made when preparing ground for the enlargement of Ditchling Churchyard, the workmen came upon an ancient well, the upper portion of which, to a depth of about 8 feet, was steined with flints, below this a lining of hewn chalk, then blocks of hewn sandstone to the bottom, 22 feet. The blocks were well cut and fitted. When the well was cleared out, some antlers and bones were found, and pronounced to be those of fallow deer. The absence of any brickwork in the well seemed to point to its ancient origin. Its situation was not far from what was once the old Rectory Barn, where former incumbents of Ditchling were wont to store their tithes, when the same were paid in kind, and probably it had been used as the well of the old Rectory House, as remains of foundations (presumed to be of this house) were also discovered in levelling the ground.

It seems curious that at the present day all trace of the boundaries of the Royal Park are obliterated, and we look in vain for "pales, limits, or enclosures" of any kind, and at what period these were removed is not known, but such names as Park Farm, Park Barn, Park Corner, Lodge Farm, Lodge Hill, and other names still linger to remind us that "Kings hunted there."

CHAPTER III.

AN ANCIENT MANSION AND ITS TENANTS.

WE now propose to treat of one of the most interesting periods in the history of Ditchling, a time in which the name of Anne of Cleves prominently figures, and round whose name and personality, local history and tradition have cast a halo of romance.

There are few people who are not acquainted with the history of this badly treated princess, at least subsequent to her arrival in England. Jane Seymour, the third wife of Henry VIII., had been dead but a few weeks ere that monarch again began to contemplate matrimony.

Of his strange infatuation with a portrait of Anne, painted by Holbein, and which must certainly have been a very flattering one, since the original is said to have been so very unlike it, we have all heard. The contract of marriage having been signed at Dusseldorf, Anne's native city, September 4th, 1539, and all preliminary matters being settled, a month later she bade farewell to her own country for ever, and set out for England, attended by a splendid retinue. She was received in this country with great pomp and ceremony, but alas, when the King saw her, we are told that he "recoiled in bitter disappointment," for the Princess was not the lovely vision which Holbein's pencil had conjured up for him. He kept up a show of civility towards his affianced wife, however, and in due course their marriage was solemnised; but after five months the union was pronounced null and void, and both parties free to wed again. From thenceforward the ex-Queen was always known as the Lady Anne of Cleves, and was endowed with estates to the value of £3,000

THE ANCIENT HOUSE.

a year, Henry "graciously adopting her for a sister," and promising that she should have precedence before all ladies of the Court, except his new consort and the Princesses Mary and Elizabeth.

After her divorce, Anne resided principally at the Palace of Richmond, but she also spent a considerable time at her various houses in Sussex, in which county considerable lands and manors had been granted for the maintenance of her rank. Her possessions in Ditchling we have already noted in dealing with the Manors. She also held the Great Tithes of Ditchling, as well as the advowson of the living, which she presented to three Vicars in succession.

But beyond her possessions in the parish whose history we are considering, she also held the neighbouring Manors of Falmer and Preston, and seems to have displayed a decided partiality for this part of the country. We believe there still hangs in one of the rooms of Preston Manor House a portrait of her, but whether Holbein's we cannot say; the room is said to have been her bedchamber. The following interesting fact may also be related concerning her connection with Preston:—

Many of our readers have doubtless seen those curious one-storied buildings which were erected some years ago by the eminent Shakspearean scholar the late J. O. Halliwell Phillips, Esq., about a mile and a quarter from Brighton, on the old road to Ditchling, and a short distance north of the old Toll House.

This latter was pulled down some years since, but those who know the spot will remember that at this point a road branches off on the right hand (going from Brighton) into a copse, now familiarly known as Hollingbury Copse, from its proximity to the Roman Encampment of that name, which is but a stone's throw distant; but in the plan which accompanied the deed for conveying the adjacent land into the possession of Halliwell Phillips, when about to build his bungalow residence, it is described as "Anne of Cleves Copse," and it is said, and doubtless with truth, that the spot was a favourite resort of that noble lady and her maidens, when staying at Preston. And now to describe what is believed to have been once the Palace of Anne of Cleves at Ditchling.

The visitor cannot fail to notice it on his first arrival, and will at once be impressed with its old time and picturesque appearance; a place which one may see has a romantic history, extending over a period of at least five hundred years.

The building, which has a very beautiful appearance with its projecting upper story and gable front and diamond pane windows, is now divided up into tenements. It is probably only a fragment of the original mansion, and a very tangible tradition exists of buildings of a like character having given place to the modern houses which adjoin. That these original houses extended all the way to the one still standing at the junction of South Street and West Street appears to admit of very little doubt, but at the same time it will be noticed that this latter, which our artist has happily named "An Old Corner," does not exhibit the same external beauty and striking features which deservedly recommend its neighbour to our notice.

All the ancient buildings, which gave way for modern ones, are traditionally believed to have been connected with the Royal residence. We do not mean to assert that they formed one large mansion, but we believe that in stating that all this area was occupied by houses and other buildings belonging to the Royal residence, we are stating a fact.

Our theory with regard to the ancient building is this: It will be seen that a considerable portion of the house stands out beyond the main building, and is now used as a workshop. A glance will show even the most casual observer that this was the main entrance, the doorway opening which has been blocked up, and a rough light put in, being easily traced in the masonry; moreover, the iron hooks on which the heavy door was hung are still to be seen fixed in the brickwork. This, then, was the entrance, and probably it was in the centre of the mansion—that is to say, rather less than two-thirds of the original house remain, a portion corresponding to that on the west side having been demolished from the east side.

Although the house has been divided up, and therefore the original character of the rooms greatly altered, what is believed to be the original staircase remains; it is a winding one, and the treads and risers are of oak, and there are many peculiar nooks and corners in various parts of the building.

Here, then, it was that the Lady Anne of Cleves, released from the perfidious Henry, far from Court intrigue, and wisely abstaining from politics, sometimes settled her well-ordered household, and here, we have no doubt, dispensed that charity for which she became noted. Holinshed says:—

"She was a lady of right commendable regard, courteous, gentle, a good housekeeper, and very bountiful to her servants."

We hear of neither quarrels, dissensions, nor plots in her little court, which she governed wisely and well, being tenderly beloved by her domestics and dependents, and surely the Lady Anne of Cleves might well be content to pass much of her time in the tranquil seclusion of her Palace at Ditchling. Her fate was indeed a happy one compared with that of the unfortunate Katherine Howard, who had supplanted her, and who in turn she saw deposed, not to retire into seclusion, as she had been permitted to do, but to suffer a shameful death. Perhaps it was while here that the news of the death of the tyrant, Henry himself, reached her; who can tell?

It has been our lot to gaze from one of the upper windows at the back of this old house, on a calm and tranquil summer evening, and we have wondered what changes the hand of time has wrought in the surrounding landscape, since the day when its former noble tenant was wont to look upon it.

Time has dealt kindly with Ditchling, and over that fair valley which stretches away from the town to the South Downs, few changes have passed; even now as our delighted vision dwells upon it, we note how like a park it appears, and in the time of Anne of Cleves, a park it was. The expanse is well wooded to this day, and retains many of the features which it anciently possessed, only requiring a few deer to complete the illusion, and persuade us that we gaze upon a scene which in three or four hundred years has not changed, and to help this illusion we have the hills, with their graceful lines, their beautiful slopes and smoothly rounded hollows and coombs, which are not changed except for an occasional pit from whence the chalk has been quarried, and which shows up spotlessly white in contrast with the greensward.

Amid such scenes as this we may imagine the Lady Anne passed the tranquil years of her life, until at a comparatively early age she was compelled to lay it aside. She died at her Palace, at Richmond, July 19th, 1557, at the age of 41, 17 years after her divorce, and having survived her faithless husband eight. Though a Protestant when she came to England, it is said that she died in communion with the Church of Rome. Her last appearance at any court ceremony was at the coronation of Queen Mary, with whom and the Princess Elizabeth she was always on excellent terms. Her tomb is in Westminster Abbey.

Another tenant of the interesting old house was Henry Poole, Esquire, who probably succeeded the Lady Anne of Cleves in the occupation thereof. This gentleman was tenant of the Royal Park of Ditchling. His once elaborate monument (now sadly mutilated) stands in the north transept of the church, but a description of this, and some extracts from his will, are given in our notes on monumental inscriptions in following pages.

Coming down to more modern times, we find the house was long occupied by the Browne family, and was known about the beginning of the last century as "Place House," but when or how it derived its present name, "Wing's Place,"* we have not been able to discover."

In a room in the Archæological Society's Quarters at Lewes, devoted almost entirely to water-colour sketches of picturesque spots in Sussex, is a water-colour of this old house, by W. H. Brooke, dated 1820, and bearing the legend, "Ancient Manor House, at Ditchling, formerly belonging to Poole family," and a later one by G. Earp, junr., about 1850. Both of these artists portray the house much in the condition that we see it to-day.

On Wednesday, June 27th, 1894, "Wing's Place" was put up and sold by auction, at the King's Head, Horsham. The agent or auctioneers thus advertised the property on their notices of the sale:—

"Lot 3. West Street. In the Village of Ditchling, Sussex, an Ancient Mansion (now let in tenements) of great Historical and Antiquarian interest, known as 'Wing's Place,' said to have been built by King Alfred the Great, and believed to be described in Doomsday Book, but the Vendors do not guarantee the accuracy of these statements; together with a garden of nice light soil. The Property is copyhold, held of the Lord of the Manor of Ditchling by an annual Quit Rent of 2d. Heriot 6d., certain on death or surrender, and a fine of 6d. on admission."

Much as we revere the ancient mansion, and would even claim for its age four or five centuries, we regret we cannot find any evidence to lead us to the conclusion

---

* "Wing's Croft" is mentioned 40th Elizabeth, 1598, but some maintain that the old ruin discovered near Lodge Farm and previously mentioned was the Palace and not Wing's Place.

that it dates back to the time of King Alfred, and the vendors of the property did well in not guaranteeing their statements to be absolutely correct with regard to its age. This legend, however, is only one of many connected with the place, and is almost as good as the one we heard a short while since, when we enquired of an inhabitant the origin of the name, "Wing's Place," and were told that it was originally Winn's, so named from a "Miss" Winn, who lived there in the days of William the Conqueror, and moreover, that that monarch used to visit her there, and subsequently married her ! !

AN OLD CORNER.

CHAPTER IV.

Old Inhabitants.

It is an easy matter to collect notes and make copious extracts for our subject, but it is a difficult task to arrange our notes in an interesting form, and the reader will forgive if, in our anxiety to interest, we depart somewhat from the beaten track usually pursued by the compilers of local histories.

In an article in Vol. xxv. of the Sussex Archæological Collections, are extracts from the diary of Mr. Marchant, of Little Park Hurst.

This gentleman was a nephew of Richard Turner, owner of the Oldland estate in 1690, and was a frequent visitor at Ditchling, and several very interesting entries relating to that place occur in the diary, and these we have selected, and they are as follows:—

October 2nd, 1716. "I was at a fair at Ditchling Common and bought 8 runts of John Jones at £25 4s., and paid him for them."

March 25, 1717. "'Lady day' Ditchling Fair and a wet day."

May 16th, 1717. Sunday. "The singers went to Ditchling in the afternoon."

The singers which are meant were those from the Parish Church at Hurst, and they probably went to assist at a service at Ditchling Church.

October 9th, 1720. "My uncle Turner was buried at Ditchling. He died last Sunday. Mr. Iver (Vicar of Ditchling) preached his funeral sermon. I was at the funeral."

This was the funeral of Richard Turner, before mentioned, who lies in a vault beneath the chancel of Ditchling, with other members of the family.

January 28th, 1721. "My wife at my aunt Turner's at Ditchling."

40 THE HISTORY OF DITCHLING.

July 16th, 1721. Sunday. "My wife and I at Ditchling to see my cousin Nicholas Marchant's widow, who is ill. We were at church and afterwards at my Aunt Turner's. Mr. Porter of Chailey preacht. Mr. Ivers being sick."

July 23, 1721. Sunday. "I was at Clayton Church in the forenoon and dined at Mr. Price's, went to Ditchling afterwards to see my cousin Marchant and was at Oldland after that."

Another entry records the sequel to the note, "Mr. Ivers being sick.' That gentleman had gone the way of all flesh.

October 30th, 1721. "At Ditchling with my wife to see Mr. Iver's goods and bought as much as came to 15s. 3d., for which I paid Mr. Nathaniel Osborne. Dined at my cousin Marchant's."

November 1st, 1721. "At Mr. Iver's sale."

December 16, 1721. "My cousin, Turner's wife of Oldland dined here" (Hurst).

March 25, 1727. "Went to Ditchling Fair. Carried Nanny behind me. We drank tea with my cousin R. Turner. Mr. R. Masters and two of the Burtenshaws were there."

This entry calls up a picture of pillion riding, and the names Masters and Burtenshaw remind us that they are those of two old Sussex families. It seems strange that in noting the fairs at Ditchling, Mr. Marchant gives them as taking place on March 25th and October 2nd, in the one case eleven days and the other ten days earlier than the dates which have been quoted as those on which these events took place, viz., April 5th and October 12th.

It will be noticed that the extracts we have given from Mr. Marchant's diary are all prior to the year 1752, and the change in the date seems to have been brought about by the alteration in the almanack.

It was in the year 1752 that by Act of Parliament this country adopted the Gregorian, or new style of reckoning time, and the calendar was adjusted by leaving out eleven days of the month of September, the 3rd day of that month being reckoned as the 14th, the eleven days which were "jumped" representing the time which had been lost in the lapse of centuries through the calendar not being exactly adjusted to the earth's orbit round the sun.

This seems to account for the alteration in the date of the fair, formerly held on Lady Day, March 25th, for if eleven days be added we shall find it becomes April the 5th, so that the Ditchling people would seem to have adhered to the old Lady Day, though the date was altered.

With regard to the other fair, we shall find if eleven days be added it will give us October 13th instead of the 12th, but it seems probable that the fair which Mr. Marchant speaks of visiting on October 2nd was not the same as that which was afterwards held on the 12th, the latter being for pedlary, and taking place in the High Street, while he speaks of it as a cattle fair, and held at Ditchling Common, so that there seems every reason to believe they were different institutions.

The early annals of Sussex history are singularly free from records of atrocious crimes and tragedies, which were few and far between, but one of the most terrible and dastardly crimes which have ever taken place in this county occurred in the parish of Ditchling on the evening of the 26th May, 1734.

The scene of the tragedy was at the Royal Oak Inn, on the northern borders of Ditchling Common, an open, dreary, and desolate waste, infested with highwaymen and footpads. The landlord at this period was a certain Richard Miles, a man well known in the district, and local tradition tells us that his house was well patronised by travellers. The inmates of the house seem to have been Richard Miles, his wife Dorothy, and a maid. To this house of entertainment came Jacob Harris, a Jew pedlar, and frequently lodged there. On the day of the tragedy he seems to have delayed his arrival until late in the evening, when all had gone, and there was no one about except the host, Mrs. Miles and the maid having already retired to bed.

Harris arrived on horseback, and the inn-keeper took charge of the animal, and led it away to the stable to clean and feed it. The pedlar followed, and while the host was engaged in attending to the animal, seized the opportunity to attack him. A struggle ensued, Miles was overpowered and the pedlar cut his throat with a razor and left him for dead. He then stealthily made for the house, but meeting the servant maid, who, it is presumed, had been aroused by the noise of the struggle he attacked and murdered her as well, then mounting to the upper part of the house where the hostess was in bed, he attacked her and cut her throat. He then plundered the house of all that was valuable, and again made his way towards the stable for the purpose of taking his horse, when, to his dismay, he discovered that he had not so effectually carried out his terrible work as he had imagined. The body of the landlord was nowhere to be seen, and excited voices in the distance told the guilty man that his victim had managed to crawl away and give the alarm. He therefore mounted his horse and made off with all speed.

The two women both died that same night, but Miles was able to give sufficient information to lead to a speedy pursuit and capture of the murderer, who was taken at Turner's Hill two or three days later, and being confronted with Miles, who lived a sufficient time to do this, was identified by him as the criminal.

The following entry, relating to the history of this crime, appears in the register of Wivelsfield Parish Church:—

"Richard Miles an Dorithy his wife murdered an was Buried hear June ye 1, 1734."

Jacob Harris was committed to gaol, and being tried

THE HISTORY OF DITCHLING. 43

at the next Horsham Assizes in August, was condemned to the gallows, and suffered for his crime at that place. His dead body was afterwards conveyed to the scene of the crime, and hung in chains on a gibbet near to the house in which the murders were committed. The history of this crime is set forth in a local rhyme of some sixty-two lines, of which we give the few concluding ones. They run as follows:—

> "At Horsham gallows, he was hanged there
> The thirty-first of August in that same year,
> And where he did the crime they took the pains
> To bring him back and hang him up in chains
> That there he might be seen by all that passed by
> It is a dismal sight for to behold
> Enough to make a heart of stone turn cold."

And truly must it have been "a dismal sight to all that passed by." But the ghastly gibbet with its clanking chains and bleaching bones was a common enough sight in the eighteenth century, when many such an one as Jacob Harris was exhibited as a warning to all evil doers.

The original gibbet gradually decayed and disappeared, until only an old rotten stump remained. This has of late years been replaced by another to mark the spot, which has ever since the crime been known as "Jacob's Post." A figure of a rooster perches on the top of it, and the date, 1734, is perforated in the metal of which the bird is composed. It is the only spot so marked in Sussex.

A fragment of the original post carried in the pocket was formerly considered a sovereign remedy for toothache, and indeed for other ills, as the following anecdote will show:—

"So recently as 1881 a Local Doctor being called to a man who was in an epileptic fit, was told by an old man (a native of Newick) 'Ah! sir, pity sure a lye, he 'adn't a bit of Jacob's Poist in his pocket!'

"'Why so?' the Doctor replied.

"'Why, don't 'ee know, sir, they do say no one wouldn't never 'ave this yere faulin sickness if he 'ad a bit o' Jacob's Poist loike about 'im. Whoy, sir, people comes *moils* and *moils*, from round Ashdown Forest way, to get a bit of dat poisty, so as they shouldn't faul wiv these yer fits.'"

No wonder was it that the post diminished when people came "moils and moils" to splinter it up into fragments as charms for all the evils that flesh is heir to.

And while touching on the subject of bodily ailments, we may mention that we have found many references to that terrible scourge smallpox, which simply raged in Sussex about the middle of the 18th century. It was a common practice at that time for persons to be inoculated and "conducted through the distemper" at the houses of medical men. Among the earliest of such practitioners whom we read of, was Dr. Cooper Sampson, of Ditchling, who, in 1758, and several subsequent years, made known to the world by means of the "Sussex Weekly Advertiser," his great success as an inoculator, "not one of his patients having any bad symptoms which are usual in the natural smallpox."

The worthy doctor's fee was four guineas, he "finding all manner of necessaries, or if patients chuse to find their own wine, tea, and sugar, three and a half guineas." He further informed the public that he was "to be spoke with every Saturday at the White Horse and Verral's Coffee House in Lewes," at the Inns of various places in the county; and at those in Brighthelmstone every Thursday where messages are taken in."

Dr. Cooper Sampson must have done well out of inoculation, for in two seasons, 1760 and 1761, he inoculated in 33 different places in Sussex 92 persons.

We regret that beyond these facts we have not been

THE HISTORY OF DITCHLING. 45

able to discover anything else relating to this funny old doctor, and cannot even locate whereabouts in the ancient town he had his dwelling where " persons were conducted through the distemper."

The following impressions (one, by a noted traveller) of Ditchling at about this period serve to show that the place is very little altered, although nearly a century and a half have passed away since Dr. Cooper Sampson flourished there.

In Bishop Pococke's MSS. account of his visit to Sussex in 1764, preserved in the British Museum, is an interesting note on Ditchling. Richard Pococke, who was a great traveller, was born at Southampton about 1704, his father being headmaster of the Free School in that town. He went to Corpus Christi College, Oxford, and took his LL.B. in 1731, and LL.D. in the same year. Subsequently he became domestic chaplain to the Earl of Chesterfield, Lord Lieutenant of Ireland. He became Bishop of Meath in 1765, and died of apoplexy in September of the same year.

In travelling through Sussex, the Bishop seems to have approached Ditchling from Cuckfield, which he describes as "a small town situated on an eminence which commands an extensive view of the country." He said, "I came seven miles to Ditchelling, the soil being more on the clay, mixed with a red flint. Though the houses and church are built of brick and flint, yet they have free stone which they will not be at the trouble of raising. Ditchelling is near the foot of the hills. It is a very small town, ten miles from Steyning, and eight from Lewes. I saw to the South (sic) Hurstpierpoint."

But the Bishop seems to have jumped rather hastily to a conclusion respecting the freestone to be found in Ditchling. We venture to assert that the sandstone is not suitable for building purposes, and except as sand it has never been quarried, having too much of a crumbling nature ; but it has been dug for sand " time out of mind," and there are a good many pits in and about Ditchling. The farm buildings hard by the church are built in a large disused sand pit; the back premises of the adjoining houses bear witness that many hundreds of tons of sand have been excavated from the site and carted away in years gone by, and it may be interesting to note that much of the sand used in building Clayton Tunnel was supplied from Ditchling and neighbourhood.

In April, 1780, the Rev. Mr. Morgan, Rector of Street, wrote of Ditchling thus:—

"The Chatfields in this parish are people of good property, particularly Mr. Michael Chatfield of Court Farm, but I believe of no family. Being Dissenters they are not entered in the Parish Register. The rest of the inhabitants of this parish are chiefly farmers and industrious tradesmen. This place is noted for Dissenters of almost all denominations. It lies under the South Downs, 7 miles West of Lewes and 7 miles North of Brighthelmstone."

As the Chatfields " of Bedyles in Ditchlyng " entered a pedigree of five descents at the Visitation of Sussex in 1574, and as the Chatfields of Oving, on entering their pedigree in 1634, acknowledged the Chatfields of Ditchling descended from Richard (whom Berry in his " Sussex Genealogies " calls Nicholas) as the senior branch of the family, Mr. Morgan's belief that they were of " no family " does not appear to have been the result of enquiry.

Of this ancient Ditchling family an early ancestor was Theobald de Chattefeld, who in 1279 was witness to a charter granting lands at Cuckfield to Lewes Priory.

Of their connection with the Baptist Meeting House in Ditchling a few particulars are given in Chapter IX.

A pedigree of the family of Chatfield will be found in the appendix.

CHAPTER V.

MISCELLANEOUS NOTES.

ABOUT a century since there lived in the neighbourhood of Ditchling an old lady, who, when preparing for a journey to London (no light matter in those days), was asked by a neighbour what sort of a place she expected to find that city. She replied, "Well, I can't exactly tell, but I suppose it must be something like the busy end of Ditchling Street."

This anecdote will provoke a smile, but we must remember that a hundred years ago it was without doubt a much busier place than it is to-day. The traffic which passed through the little town from London to Brighton, and vice versa, was very considerable, for Ditchling is situated on one of the oldest turnpike roads in the district, and coaches ran through it during the last decade of the 18th century. Think of those, the high born and rich, who, in the early days of the last century, may have passed this way to Brighton, then fast rising into public favour and resorted to, we are told, by "the gay and polite." We must bear in mind, also, that in those days, and well on into the middle of the century, no railways were in existence, such a scheme as tunnelling through the broad South Downs had not even been dreamed of, and all travelling had to be done by road.

Thus it was that Ditchling, a considerable distance from Lewes and Cuckfield, and even from Hurst, its nearest neighbour of any importance, drew in from the surrounding district all the trade, or a very large proportion of it. Picture the place on a market day, it was alive with those who came to buy or sell, and what a busy scene must have been presented on the annual fair days, when the stalls were ranged on either side the street, displaying all the oddments of a country town fair.

Then there was the arrival and departure of the coaches, which rattled through the little town to change horses at the Bull Inn before climbing that terrible ascent Ditchling Borstal.

The following is an extract from "Brighton and its Coaches," by W. C. A. Blew, M.A.:—

"In 1794 there appeared for the first time an advertisement of a coach running to London through Ditchling and Lindfield, but as its anonymous proprietors stated that 'it continues running,' it must have been on the road the previous year, and possibly longer than that. She started from the White Lion and Golden Cross, Brighton, and ran to the George and Blue Boar, Holborn, leaving Brighton at eight o'clock on Monday and Friday, and returning at seven o'clock in the morning on Wednesday and Saturday, though when summer set in the coach ran thrice a week each way."

In connection with the coaches, we will record an incident which happened early in the last century, and was related to us a year or two since by a very old man, then living in Lewes, but who was a native of Ditchling, and spent his childhood there.

It was in the depth of winter, and the snow lay thick over all the country round Ditchling. There are few boys of robust health and high spirits who do not enjoy a game of snowballing, and so it happened that school being over for the day, a party of urchins betook themselves towards the north end of Ditchling, and there organised and carried out a snowball fight. They seem to have had an attacking and defending party, but the attacking party seem to have been gradually driven back to the toll gate which then existed at the northern extremity of Ditchling. The snowballing being over, they cast about for something more

THE HISTORY OF DITCHLING.

to occupy their minds and hands, and some suggested that a monster snow man should be raised in the middle of the road, but this was abandoned, as already it was dusk, and it would have taken long to complete.

Then someone literally set the ball rolling. At first a tiny thing he made to throw at one of his companions, but threw it down and rolled it in the snow, and as he rolled, so it gathered and grew, and became as large as a football. Then his companions began to push it down the road towards the town, and as they pushed it, so with every inch grew the ball as they rolled it over and over in the snow, till it became a thing so large that it required the strength of many even of those sturdy country lads to impel it onwards. Still they rolled it, and laughed and shouted as it grew ever larger and larger, and heavier and heavier. They lent all their strength to it till at last from the size of a cricket ball it had become so large as to be unmanageable, and they came to a dead stop in the middle of the road. Then they danced round the gigantic monster in a delirium of wild delight, which brought out the people on to their door steps and the blacksmith with his men to the smithy door. But even above their shouts came another sound, that of the posthorn, and round a bend in the road they discerned the lamps of the London coach, bound for Brighton, rapidly approaching.

"The coach!" went from lip to lip excitedly, and even as they said it, they noted that the gate-keeper, unaware of the enormous snowball which blocked the road, and perhaps of uncertain sight, had the gate open for the coach to pass through. On it came, and an accident seemed imminent, the gigantic monster blocked the way, the coach would be wrecked and the passengers killed. But fortunately someone had presence of mind enough to give the warning to the coachman to stop, and this he did none too soon, pulling up his leaders within but a few feet. Then followed a scene of confusion. The "insides" got out and the "outsides" got down. The horses were restive, the coachman used unparliamentary language, and the conductor boxed the ears of all the boys he could lay his hands upon.

The blacksmith and his men meanwhile began to hack away at the snowball, and gradually, after some minutes had elapsed, demolished it. Then the "insides" once more took their places, and the "outsides" took theirs. The conductor climbed up, and with a parting cut with his long whip towards those mischievous urchins, the coachman drove away down the High Street.

It would be possible to relate many such stories as the foregoing in connection with Ditchling, and here is one which seems to aptly illustrate how very much in seclusion country people were wont to live before the advent of the railways.

A certain man who was a thatcher and lived in Ditchling, seems to have very seldom wandered from the vicinity of his home, for the following facts are told concerning him.

A remarkably violent storm occurred on the 29th November, 1836, and did considerable damage to property in Sussex. At Ditchling Vicarage, a large chimney stack being blown through the roof and the rain pouring in, compelled the inmates to seek shelter in a neighbouring house.

The Brighton Chain Pier (now, alas, gone for ever) suffered considerably. Now at this time it had been built about 13 years only, and it is probable that many people living in the outlying towns and villages round Brighton had not seen the wonderful structure which was then considered—and justly so—a marvel of engineering skill, and a perfect wonder. Now, of those who had not seen it, the worthy thatcher seems to have been one, and some kind friend and practical joker, knowing this, informed him that the recent storm had "blown all the thatch off the Chain Pier," and that if he went there he would be sure to get "a good job," *and he went.*

Can we not imagine the "Silly Sussex?" He had not the remotest idea of what that beautiful pier was like, and so he gathered up his tools and trudged off over the Beacon to Brighton, only to find when he arrived at the Pier that the structure before him with its graceful curves and its iron chains and towers was not "a thatched one," and that he had been most decidedly "sold." It would be interesting to know how he settled matters with his friend on his return to Ditchling, but on this point, as on so many others, history and tradition are alike silent.

Before the Police Force came into existence, it was the usual thing for people of property, and for their own safety, to band themselves together into societies.

Such a society flourished in Ditchling during the eighteenth, and well on to the middle of the nineteenth century. We have before us as we write a copy of the rules of this institution, after their revision in November, 1834. It is headed thus:—

"Ditchling Society for prosecuting thieves, etc. Held at the Bull Inn, Ditchling. In the county of Sussex. Established the 30th day of November, 1784."

The object of the society was to raise a fund for prosecuting persons who were found to be guilty of murdering or robbing and defrauding any member of the said society of their property, and for the more effectually discovering and bringing such persons to justice, and for offering and paying such rewards to persons giving information whereby such offenders were apprehended and convicted.

A meeting of this society "was held once in every year at the Bull Inn on Monday nearest the full moon in the month of November, and that dinner be upon the table at two o'clock in the afternoon, and that each member pay three shillings to defray the ordinary expenses thereof."

At this meeting all the business of the Society was transacted, and a treasurer and a clerk appointed every year.

No member, we are told, was to claim protection for any property " situated beyond ten miles from the town of Ditcheling."

The following is a list of members of the Ditchling Society in 1834:—

John Borrer, Mrs. Anne Chatfield, Jesse Kensett, Richard Mercer, and John Wood, and Mrs. Sarah Frances Thompson (all of Ditchling); Capt. W. H. Bacchus (Theobalds, Wivelsfield), Richard Tanner of Morehouse and James Hemsley of Wivelsfield, John Hollingdale, Thos. Morley of Plumpton, William Sturt (Street Place) and William Foulconer (Street), John Ede (Miller Clayton) and Thomas Dominick Whiteman of the same place; Henry Holman, William Marshall, and Richard Weeks, of Hurst, and John Hodson, of Shoreham.

In the year 1822 the first show of the Ditchling Horticultural Society was held, and this annual event, which takes place in July, is even now considered the principal social gathering of the year.

To celebrate the 38th anniversary of this " shew," for so is the word spelt in the early advertisement bills printed in Ditchling, a token was struck. We have seen one of these in a little card box in the possession of one of the inhabitants.

On the obverse side of the token we read:—

" 1860. Ditchelling XXXVIII Anniversary of the Gooseberry and Currant Show, Stool Ball match and Kettle Feast."

On the reverse:—

" 1860. Given by Mr. Thos. Attree of Brighton in the 84th year of his age."

Of the famed Ditchling Gooseberry, we feel constrained to speak. At the annual show it may be seen in all its native glory. Surely it may be said with safety that such splendid specimens as are there exhibited are not to be met with at any other place in the kingdom, and so fine are they that they have been known to sell at sevenpence each.

The Ditchling gardeners are to be complimented on the perfection to which they have attained in rearing this luscious fruit.

CHAPTER VI.

St. Margaret's Church.

DITCHLING Parish Church, occupying the commanding site which it does, rising above the surrounding houses, is a conspicuous landmark from all points of view. There is no doubt that at the period when it was erected the surrounding district was densely wooded, and the spot was selected as being peculiarly adapted to make the edifice subsequently reared, serve as a guide to the traveller and wayfarer.

Respecting the dedication there is a slight doubt, but the Patron Saint is believed to be St. Margaret, a virgin who suffered martyrdom at Antioch in the 3rd century, and who was a favourite Saint with women in the middle ages, and one especially invoked against the pains of child-birth.

We have noted in previous pages that Edward II. granted a charter for holding an annual three days' fair at the festival of the above-named Saint, and this fact alone seems almost to prove that the sacred edifice was dedicated to her.

Ditchling Church has been described by more than one writer as " one of the finest of the Sussex Hillside Churches, being just in its proportions and beautiful in its details." Quite recently a visitor described the interior as " a pleasing mixture of ancient and modern," a term which seems to aptly illustrate the general effect. And here let us say that the visitor may see but little in the exterior to commend it to his notice ; it is a plain building, giving little promise of a beautiful interior. In plan it is cruciform, and is built of flints with stone dressings, and comprises north and south chancel, a central tower, which is crowned by a low spire, north

THE CHURCH FROM THE ANCIENT HOUSE.

and south transepts, nave with south aisle, which are under the same roof, and a south porch. It is roofed with tiles and Horsham stone, while the spire is covered with oak shingles, and contains six bells and a clock.

Though the greater part of the building is considered to date from the thirteenth century, and is generally considered a fine specimen of the Early English style, the tower, transepts, and chancels exhibiting some very rich work of that period, we believe that some portions may lay claim to a much greater antiquity, for some authorities inform us that the church mentioned in Domesday Book was built by Alfred the Great, and is incorporated in the present building. This is not improbable, as traces of Saxon architecture are even now to be found, and the following discovery will prove that there was a place of sepulture here in Saxon times.

About ten years ago, some workmen were digging outside the church to form a stoke hole for the hot water apparatus. In the course of this work the men came upon an excavation formed in the sandstone rock, between the north wall of the chancel and east wall of the north transept, at a depth of about three feet from the original ground line. The sandstone had been hollowed out to about a foot in depth, and in this lay the skeleton of a man over six feet in height. The skull was of a very refined type, and the teeth were strong and sound, but the molars showed signs of gouty fissures. Not a sign was there of any coffin either of lead or wood; the remains had simply been laid in the hollow formed to receive them. It was a Saxon grave, and he who reposed there must have been a Saxon.

The admirer of architecture will find much to interest in studying this church, but we would ask the visitor before examining any details to stand at the end of the nave, or, better still, to enter by the western door, and he will at once be struck by the beautiful effect which is thus obtained. The lofty arches, with their beautiful foliated capitals, and the east window of the chancel will suggest the idea of a miniature cathedral. The tower is supported on four lofty pointed arches, and the shafts, or piers, which carry them, are trefoil in character, except those of the eastern arch, which are varied about five feet from the ground up to the capitals, seeming to suggest that the original stones have been pared down. The shafts of the chancel arch, as well as the eastern shafts of the transepts, are enriched with foliated capitals, but those of the nave arch have only a circular moulded capital.

The east window of the main chancel is divided into three pointed lights by slender shafts, terminating in foliated capitals, and has three circles above, two of which are cinquefoil and one quatrefoil, the circles having deep and rounded hollow mouldings. At the angles of the jambs are shafts supporting the window arch, which is ornamented by an ogee moulding. The shafts have bell-shaped capitals, richly ornamented with foliage. The hood moulding or label of this window terminates on one side with the head of a king, and on the other that of a queen, wearing their crowns, and are believed to represent Edward III. and his queen. These heads are remarkably well preserved, and are carved in chalk, a material which was largely used in the interior decoration of this church. On either side of the east window is a niche about two-thirds the height of the window; that on the north side has a trefoil headed ogee arch; that on the south side a cinquefoil. It is believed that these niches once contained images of Saints, and no doubt they were originally formed for that purpose. The Commandments are now written in them. In the north wall is a trefoil headed aumbry, and in the south wall a piscina and credence table, the upper part of which is Perpendicular, having probably been rebuilt at a later period. The piscina is Early English; adjoining this is a sedile.

THE HISTORY OF DITCHLING.

There are three windows on the north side of the chancel, lancet-shaped, under ogee arches, and these are also supported by slender shafts at the angles of the jambs, the capitals of which are also enriched with foliage. The splay of these windows is unusually large. The easternmost of the three has no corbel, but the other two have corbel heads at the termination of the hood moulding, carved in chalk; that on the middle window (the side nearest the altar) is believed to be the head of St. Margaret, the Patron Saint of the church (see vignette on title page).

A circular string course runs below the chancel windows, but only internally.

The priests' door in the north wall of the chancel has been closed up for many years, but the architecture of the same is worthy of attention. Its bold round and hollow mouldings are interesting in detail, and internally the carved chalk, and externally the stonework, are both remarkably well preserved.

Passing into the south chancel, or as it is now called, the Abergavenny Chapel, from the fact that it is attached to the principal Manor, we find here a 14th century chantry. It will be noticed that the east and two south windows are decorated. The former has three cusped lights, with three quatrefoils above, but no further decoration; the south windows, like those in the main chancel, have shafts to carry the arches, decorated capitals, and carved corbel heads to the hood mouldings, and each is divided into two principal lights with a quatrefoil in the head. Traces of the altar are to be found at the east end. In the south wall is the piscina, trefoil headed, but the basin is gone and has been replaced by a plain piece of stone. The chantry door has long been built up, but may be traced in the masonry. The two chancels are divided by a plain arch, but formerly under this arch was a coped wall about five feet high, in which there was an opening to give access from one chancel to the other, but this was removed when the church was restored, the south chancel being no longer a private chapel, as it had been in ancient days.

The visitor will not fail to notice the vast amount of chalk used in decorating the chancels, a material which appears in places to have stood the test of time even better than stone itself, as a glance at the mouldings, corbels, and window shafts and capitals will at once convince him. Many of these are as perfect as when the skilled artisan carved them, centuries ago, and even now they may lay claim to great beauty of style and excellent workmanship.

Turning to the south aisle, we believe we are in the oldest portion of the church. It is divided from the nave by two very plain Transition arches. They spring from three square piers, which have a plain impost, and there is no sub-arch, and nothing in the way of ornament. The piers are the remains of a Saxon Church. The south transept has one window only, the architecture of which we believe we are correct in styling debased Gothic.

The north transept was entirely rebuilt when the church was restored. It has two narrow lancet windows in the east wall, and a three-light debased Gothic window in the west wall, while a staircase in the north wall communicates with the ringing chamber and belfry.

The nave, formerly Norman, has now three decorated windows in the north wall, and one over the west doorway, all of which are modern.

Before noting what took place at the restoration of the church, which, by-the-bye, seems to have been on the whole a judicious one, we may note the following:

Hussey's "Churches of Kent, Surrey, and Sussex," published in 1852, and therefore before the restoration took place, mentions that the chancel tie beam formerly

THE HISTORY OF DITCHLING. 61

had the dog tooth moulding carved upon it, but it " was removed about fifty years ago by the lay Rector " (about the beginning of the nineteenth century). The same account also mentions a " small Norman window remaining at the west end of the aisle."

Some notes on Ditchling, Sussex, by William Hamper, published in the " Gentleman's Magazine " for 1812, describes the font as " of stone, octagonal in shaft and bason ; very plain, and not calculated for immersion."

These features have all undergone changes. The present chancel tie beam is plain, the Norman window has been replaced by one in a somewhat different style, and the font is a modern one.

Nearly forty years have now elapsed since the late Vicar, Reverend Thomas Hutchinson, formed a committee with the object of taking in hand the extensive restoration of the sacred building, a committee which, formed in 1863, had the satisfaction of seeing the whole, or nearly the whole, of the money required for carrying out the proposed work in hand before operations were commenced.

So the parishioners of Ditchling bade farewell to the old high pews and the west gallery, and betook themselves to the National School for Divine Service, until such times as the extensive repairs and alterations should be completed.

Happily, there are several views of the exterior before restoration, but it is to be regretted, so far as we are aware, none of the interior.

In Vol. xxviii., Suss. Arch. Coll., appears an illustration of the church in 1780, taken from the southeast.

The " Gentleman's Magazine " for 1812 has an illustration of the exterior.

The late R. H. Nibbs also made a sketch of the same.

At the headquarters of the Sussex Archæological Society, at Lewes, among the collection of water-colour sketches is one of Ditchling Church, by G. Earp, jun., dated 1850, and showing the old outside staircase to west gallery. We have also seen a pencil drawing showing the old north transept and staircase to belfry, this being in possession of one of the inhabitants. Mr. George de Paris made a study of the church from the south-west in 1856, and four others from various points at later periods, the first named, however, showing the edifice before any restoration was made. Mr. Montague Penley also made a study of the church in 1858. There are views of this church in the British Museum, among the Burrell MSS.

Amongst the alterations carried out in 1863 may be enumerated the following. The north transept entirely taken down and rebuilt; the north wall of the nave entirely taken out and rebuilt, and the three decorated windows inserted in same; the old west window taken out and a smaller decorated window put in its place; the old west gallery, in which the minstrels were wont to sit and discourse sweet music with strings and pipe, removed; the old pews taken out and the church entirely reseated in a modern style; gas introduced for lighting the church; communion table, pulpit, eagle lectern, reading desk, and font canopy, all of which are of carved oak, provided, and the sanctuary tiled with mosaics.

Like many other churches, the walls were covered with a thick coating of whitewash. This was removed, and in so doing traces of mural paintings were observed, but were too much decayed for the subject to be discerned, or to be worth preservation, so no attempt was made to do this.

When at length the restoration was complete and the church reopened for Divine Service, a feeling of satisfaction prevailed among the parishioners that the work had been so well and thoroughly carried out.

The next work attempted was to provide a clock for

INTERIOR OF THE CHURCH.

the spire, and this and other work in connection with erecting it, cost about one hundred pounds. It faces to north and south, strikes the hours and chimes the quarters. The spire underwent extensive repairs in 1897, as a memorial of Queen Victoria's Diamond Jubilee, when it was part reshingled.

And, by the way, perhaps some of our readers may not know what a " shingled spire " is, and a note in passing may not be uninteresting. Many Sussex spires, instead of being tiled, are covered with thin pieces of cleft oak, in size about 9in. by 5in. by ½in., and these are known by the name of shingles.

The word shingle seems to be derived from the Latin Scindere, viz., to cut, slash, rend, tear, or pull in pieces; to break off or divide; to split; and as the term shingle is applied to the loose stones on the sea shore, which are fragments of rock split from large masses, so in the same sense is it applied to wood split off or rent from larger pieces.

The six bells, which are of sweet tone, and are hung in the spire, are inscribed as follows :—

Nos. 1, 3 and 4. " Lester and Pack of London, fecit 1766."

No. 2. " Peace and Good neighbourhood." " Lester and Pack of London, fecit."

No. 5. " Edwd. Harraden, Thos. Field, & Jas. Wood Churchwardens, Lester & Pack of London 1766."

No. 6. " To the Glory of God and to the memory of Thomas Hutchinson, Vicar 1883." Cast by Gillett & Co. Croydon 1884.

The weight of the tenor bell is 8cwt. 2qrs. 16lbs.

The bells are always chimed at eight o'clock on Sunday morning, a custom dating back to ancient times.

It may be mentioned that the church possesses an Elizabethan chalice and patten, considered exceedingly beautiful and perfect specimens of the period, dated 1568, and also a fine old pewter flagon, on which is inscribed:—

      The Revd. Willm. Lamb Viquer.
    Edw. Harraden, ⎱   Churchwardens
    Richd. Morris   ⎰   1728.

And before closing our notes on the church, one or two traditions in connection with by-gone times may here be conveniently related.

In former days the place is said to have been noted for its singers, and there is an old couplet which has been handed down to us, and runs thus:—

"Ditchling Singers and Bolney Ringers."

Now, it is a well-known fact that till within comparatively recent years music in Sussex was at a desperately low ebb; but if we are to believe tradition, such was not the case at Ditchling, whose singers had few rivals in the surrounding villages. This was in the days of the old west galleries, and the singing was unaccompanied, the note only being given with a pitch pipe.

But, whatever may have been the heights which we would fain hope these worthy musicians aspired to in the west gallery, and to which perchance they attained, there are other stories told concerning them which would seem to show them to us in a somewhat more worldly light.

One is, that at one time they were all, without exception, smugglers. This, however, was no uncommon thing in those days, for there were few, either rich or poor, who were not, directly or indirectly, mixed up in the contraband traffic.

Another story runs thus:—

The Ditchling singers took an eventful journey to Henfield, or some other village out west, to sing at a festival. The journey was made in a cart.

Returning home, a few took the cart, leaving the

others to walk. Those in the cart made a long stay at the Shepherd and Dog, at Fulking. Here the walking party arrived, and seeing the cart outside, took possession and drove on. The party inside the inn looked upon this as a trick, and with all possible speed took a short cut across country and caught them up. Then took place a fierce fight for possession of the cart, which was a sad ending indeed to the Sunday excursion. It is said that the then Vicar of Ditchling did not venture to reproach his choir individually for their conduct, but preached a sermon the following Sunday on the text, "See that ye fall not out by the way."

A notice of Ditchling Church would be incomplete without a few words about the family of white owls which have from time immemorial made their abode in the roof of the south chancel. The habits of these birds are indeed most interesting. If unmolested they frequent the same haunt for many years, and are said to prefer towns and villages rather than more secluded places in which to rear their young, and at times become wonderfully tame. They are great destroyers of vermin; moles, rats, shrews, and mice forming their prey, and sometimes small birds, such as larks and sparrows, and they are not averse to beetles and other kinds of insects. They seldom fly by day, unless in the dull days of winter time, and if by chance they are disturbed from their haunts, fly about in a desultory manner.

Years ago, when some repairs were in progress to the roof of the south chancel, a curious circumstance happened. A scaffold was erected to enable the workmen to do the necessary repairs, and the owls, disturbed by this, betook themselves into the adjoining roof of the main chancel. The roof of their former abode was then stripped of the tiling, and between the apex and the wood panelling was found an enormous quantity of refuse, which had been accumulated in the course of many years. This consisted principally of skeletons and pellets, and when removed amounted to many barrows full.

Meanwhile, the owls complacently watched the renovation of their old home, and after rearing their young where—as the sequel proved—they had only temporarily taken up their abode, returned to their former quarters when the repairs were finished, and where their descendants still flourish.

A tranquil summer evening is the best time to observe this bird. It comes from under the eaves of the roof, and with graceful and noiseless flight goes to seek its prey, and after hovering over a small area, it suddenly swoops down to the earth, clutches the prey in its claw, and makes towards home, this being repeated a number of times.

The note of the white owl is a screech. It seldom or never hoots, and the odd kind of snoring noise so plainly audible on a summer evening is made by the young, and seems to be a call to their parents for food.

We can recall an occasion on which one of these interesting birds penetrated to the interior of the church, beneath the roof of which its kind have so long found sanctuary. It was at evensong. From one of the circles of the east window, standing on one leg and with the other drawn up into its thick plumage, and with head awry, it inquisitively watched the assembling of the congregation. Later it changed its position, and hopped on to the tie beam, from which point of vantage it intently regarded the white-robed figures of the choir below, until finally, at intervals during the service, it flew from end to end of the church in a noiseless and graceful manner.

DITCHLING VICARAGE IN THE YEAR 1820.

CHAPTER VII.

ECCLESIASTICAL NOTES—RECTORS AND VICARS OF DITCHLING.

THE Rectory of Ditchling was originally in the patronage of the de Warennes up to the thirteenth century, at which time it was appropriated to the Priory of St. Pancras in Lewes, the Prior and monks of which institution thereby became rectors and patrons of the living, and appointed the Vicar (their nominee) to it, giving him the small tithes, and themselves retaining the great. This continued so until the suppression of the monasteries in the reign of Henry VIII., when that monarch, instead of giving back the church's own, sold the great tithes of the parish and advowson (that is patronage of the living) to whoever would buy either the one or the other. Anciently, the neighbouring parish of Wivelsfield was annexed to Ditchling for several centuries. In a charter from Seffrid II. (Bishop of Chichester, 1180-1204) to the Monastery of St. Pancras, Lewes, Wivelsfield is mentioned as a chapel of ease to Ditchling, and in all early documents relating to the latter place, the invariable description is "Dychenyng, with the chapel of Wivelsfield annexed."

This arrangement came to an end during the fifteenth century, when the two churches were separated, and Wivelsfield made an independent parish under the control of another Vicar. It is interesting to note, however, that although thenceforward the two parishes were no longer united, several of the Vicars of Ditchling, which may be considered the mother church, also presided over the parish of Wivelsfield.

There is a record of another chapel somewhere in Ditchling as early as the year 1200, but as this chapel is not mentioned after 1290, it is perhaps more probably the chapel of Wivelsfield mentioned above, although the charter of Seffrid mentions the " Church of Ditcheninge with the chapel of Wivelsfield," and the reference in Hussey's " Churches of Kent, Sussex, and Surrey," and Horsfield's " Lewes," II., App IV., is the " Church of Falmere with the Chapel of Burgmeria, Chapel of Swanbergh of Horsted ; of Ditcheninge and of Belandre and of Lameria, of Stedham with the Chapel of Hedser, the Church of Petworth, with the Chapel of Buddington, the Church of Tullington and of Coate," from which it appears doubtful whether the church or the chapel of Ditchling is meant.

In the year 1352, the living, with others, was changed for the Church of Birton by the Prior and Convent of Lewes, but they must have acquired it again, for we learn that during the episcopate of Richard Mitford (1390), a dispute arose as to the patronage of the church of Ditchling with that of Wivelsfield annexed, and also of two other churches in the neighbourhood, and it was decided by him (the Bishop), on the question being referred to him for settlement, that such patronage was vested in the religious establishment of St. Pancras at Lewes.

With the dissolution and destruction of this monastery, in the reign of Henry VIII., came an alteration.

The Lady Anne of Cleves became patroness of the living of Ditchling, and impropriatress of the rectorial tithes. Subsequently they passed into the possession of the Michelbournes, an old Sussex family, described as being of Broadhurst and Stanmer in this county, and owners of Oldland in Keymer, where some of the family are said to have resided in the reign of Henry VIII.

The arms of this family were Or, a cross, between four eagles, displayed sable, and their crest, on a wreath, or and azure, a tiger passant, and were first granted in 1571, November 1st, the original grant adding five wolves or, on the cross, but in a few cases only do the family appear to have borne these.

An early alias of this family was Mascall. "Michelborne, alias Mascall," is a name which often occurs in deeds, etc., of the 15th century.

Their descent may be traced from one "Thomas Michelborne of Lyndfield," in the reign of Edward IV., whose grandson, John Michelbourne, of Westmeston, married Joane, daughter of Richard Hether, of Ditchling, by whom he had issue, Richard Michelbourne, of Horsted Keynes and Ditchling, who died April 29th in the 25th year of Elizabeth, and whose son Richard, of Broadhurst, married Agnes, daughter and co-heiress of Christopher Turke, of Fletching, by Joan his wife, daughter of Richard AtRee, of Theobalds in Wivelsfield.

This lady predeceased her husband; she died June 14th, 1597, and he October 16th, 1607. They were both buried at Ditchling, presumably in the chancel. Their son, Sir Richard Michelbourne, of Broadhurst and Stanmer, was Sheriff of Surrey and Sussex 18 Jac I., and died and was buried at Horsted Keynes, 18th September, 1638.

He it was who sold the Rectorial Tithes of Ditchling in 1637 to Thomas Turner, grandson of John Turner, who in the last year of Henry VIII. had purchased Oldland, in Keymer, of the Michelbournes. Thomas Turner was the ancestor of numerous descendants throughout the county of Sussex, for by his wife, whose maiden name was Smythe, he had twenty-three children. The elder branch of the family resided at Oldland for many generations, and the principal members are buried in the vaults of the chancel at Ditchling, where they had obtained the right of sepulture.

From the Turners the great tithes passed to the Attree family, the representatives of whom are the present impropriators or lay rectors. The impropriate tithes are valued at £500 gross. We may note that the male line of the family of Michelbourne became extinct in 1721 by the death of Colonel John Michelbourne.

In the register of Pyecombe, there is a note signed Edward Bland, Rector, stating that the corn tithes of Lower Standean, in Ditchling Parish, were given to the rectory of Pyecombe at the dissolution.

During Archbishop Whitgift's primacy, he addressed a letter to Anthony Watson, Bishop of Chichester 1596-1605, desiring him to ascertain among other items " The certaine number of those who do receive the communion in everie several parishe." The results of these enquiries have only been preserved in a few instances, but amongst them we find the number of communicants at Ditchling was 200.

Of the several charities belonging to the parish of Ditchling, the most important is that known as " Sprotts." The foundress of this charity was probably " Isabell Sprot," spinster, who was residing in Ditchling in the year 1378, when the poll tax of Richard II. was taken. As this is the only notice of the name in any record yet discovered, there seems little doubt that she was the foundress of the charity. The income is derived from lands, and amounting to about fifty pounds yearly, is, with the exception of one pound deducted for church repairs, divided amongst those poor people of Ditchling who have not during the past year received " parochial relief." The Tithe Map, dated 1797, indicates the name, position, and acreage of the various pieces of land from which the income of Sprotts is derived, viz., Burnt Inholmes (2), Brooms Croft, Beggars Bush, Marlpit, Alms Croft, Church Croft, Common Fields (2), Flat Field, Green Meadow, Milking Croft, the whole comprising an area of about thirty-five acres.

A law case connected with this charity, extending from about 1767 to 1783, cost about £460.

The various deeds bear the following dates: 156$\frac{8}{9}$, 1601, 1636, 1661, 1665, 1677, 1781, 1832.

Another charity, known as Lucas's, of the annual value of £2 12s., was formerly expended in bread, and distributed on the first Sunday in each month.

Beyond these charities are the Boddington Trust, £150, and the Dorrell Trust, £50, the joint interest of which amounts to about five pounds yearly, distributed to eleven deserving poor of the parish, the first named having been bequeathed by the late Miss Mary Ann Boddington and the last by the late Mr. Dorrell, who for some years prior to his death had spent the summer months in Ditchling.

The Burrell MSS. give 1551 as the year in which the parish registers of Ditchling commence, but in reality the earliest dates extant are as follows:—

The earliest baptism is dated 19th February, 1557.

The earliest marriage is dated 1st February, 1556.

The earliest burial is dated 15th October, 1556.

As the baptism and marriage years are 1557-8 and 1556-7 respectively, the earliest entry is the burial one.

The following are some of the old family names which appear in the registers, most of them during the 16th century:—

Godman, Godlye, Attree, Amore, Undrell, Awode, Markwick, Beard, Fayrell, Michelbourne, Pollington, Poole, Haslegrove, Gatland, Shelley, Standen, Pardone, Chatfield, Hubbard (sometimes written Ubbard), Marchant, Colstocke, Willett, Cheale, Burton, Moore, Scrase, Turner, Wood.

The houses known as "Pardons," "Cheals," and "Colstock," still existing in Ditchling at the present day, were doubtless the homes of the respective families bearing these names.

The churchwardens' accounts commence in 1638, and are continued down to the present time in a very perfect manner.

Mr. Edmund Attree, churchwarden in 1638, was of Theobalds, in Wivelsfield, and died at Wivelsfield in 1660. A list of the names of those who held office down to 1750 will be found among the appendices.

The ecclesiastical living of Ditchling is now a vicarage, the gross income being valued at £321, with a house.

The vicarage house dates from about the reign of Charles I., but has of late years been added to several times.

The following is a list of the Rectors and Vicars of Ditchling with Wivelsfield.

Admitted.	Rectors.	How Vacant.
1279	Theobald de la Bell	
1310	Edmund de Newington	
1324	Nicholas Burnell	
1366	John Vincent	
1382	John de Chitterne	
1382 Oct. ...	William Brompton	

Admitted.	Vicars.	How Vacant.
1415 r ...	Richard Ayleboyne	
1415	John Sale	
1416	Richard Croseby	
1442 r ...	John Chapman	
1442 Dec. 20	John Rysshton ...	res John Chapman.
1444 Dec. 15	Ralph Wode	res John Rysshton.
1478	Robert Funderhay	
1513 d ...	Richard Feyrher	
1513 Aug. 4	John Geymyshe ...	d Richard Feyrher.
1514 Feb. 13	Sampson Michael...	d John Geymyshe.
1534 Dec. 28	John Coke	res Sampson Michael
1552 Apr. 20	John Rose (Clerk)	de John Coke.
1552 Oct. 7	John Ferriss	de John Rose.
1554 Sep. 22	Thomas Gurnell ...	dep John Ferriss.
1565 June 9	Humfry Higgons	
1566 Jan. 16	Edward Linfield ...	d Humfry Higgons.
1566	Thos. Harris (Clerk)	
1568-9... ...	Edward Peckham.	

THE HISTORY OF DITCHLING.

Admitted.	Vicars.	How Vacant.
1573	Edward Richards.	
	Thomas Bridgeman	d Edward Peckham.
1581	Edward Denton ...	Perhaps as Curate on death of T. Bridgeman.
1583 Aug. 22	Henry Pye	
	Edward Denton (as Vicar),	
1589 Apr. 26	Hugh Rawood ...	res Edward Denton.
1604 July 31	Anthony Mattock...	d Hugh Rawood.
1606 June 18	Thomas Price ...	res Anthony Mattock.
1621	Mascall Giles ...	d Thomas Price.
1645 to 1647	John Buckley ...	Parliamentary intruders probably not ordained.
1649 to 1650	Samuel Snell... ...	
1653 to 1658	Edward Lulham ...	
1662 to 1664	John Gravett.	
1664 Aug. 15	John Crump, A.M.	
1666 Jan. 9	William Willys.	
1674 Mar. 30	John Parker	d William Willys.
1692 July 30	John Nicholls	
*1715 Aug. 10	Elnathan Iver, B.A.	d John Nicholls.
*1721 Dec. 11	William Lamb ...	d Elnathan Iver.
*1740	Edward Powell	
1746 June 3	Daniel Walter ...	de Edward Powell.
1746-7 Mar. 3	Samuel Jefferies ...	cess Daniel Walter.
1777 May 16	Joseph Bailey ...	d Samuel Jefferies.
*1794 Sep. 5	John Hanley, A.M.	d Joseph Bailey.
*1795 May 19	Thos. Hudson, LL.B.	cess John Hanley.
1820 Mar. 27	Denny Ashburnham	
1843 Sep. 28	Julius Nouaille, A.B.	d Denny Ashburnham.
1855 Apr. 16	Thomas Hutchinson, M.A.... ...	d Julius Nouaille.
1883 Dec. ...	Francis Collins Norton	d Thomas Hutchinson.

* Those marked * also perpetual curates of Wivelsfield.

PATRONS.

1310 Prior and Convent of Lewes.
1552 Lady Anne of Cleves.
1612 Henry Hider, Gent.
1664 Chancellor of Chichester.
1777 Thomas Williams.

The living is now vested in trustees.

Wivelsfield became a separate parish in 1478, when William Clarke became perpetual curate or chaplain.

A few extracts from the registers and notes from various other sources with regard to the above gentlemen may be of interest.

In the subsidy granted the first year of Edward III. (1327), the Rector of Ditchling (Nicholas Burnell) paid the sum of two shillings.

The fifth on the list, John de Chitterne, exchanged his living, 28th October, 1382, with William Brompton, who is described as "Parson of New Church, Isle of Wight."

Humfry Higgons seems to have formerly been Rector of Newick, having been appointed to that living October 20, 1559. Edward Linfield (1566) seems to have gone to Framfield, or he may have held that living as well as Ditchling, a man of the same name having been inducted to that parish May 6, 1569. Henry Pye's Vicariate lasted only six months. He went to Peasemarsh April 11, 1584.

Extracts from Registers:—

1569 Aug. 14	Francis s Edward Peckham Bap.	
1574 June 3	Edward Peckham Vicar, bur.	
1575 Dec. 23	Edward Denton & Rebecca Stanford, mar.	
1576 Dec. 9	Edward s Edward Dentone, bap.	
158$\frac{0}{1}$ Feb. 19	Thomas Bridgeman, Vicar, bur.	
,, Mar. 22	Dorithie, d Edward Dentone, bap.	
158$\frac{3}{4}$ Feb. 19	Constance d ,, ,, ,,	
1586 Apr. 14	Thomas s ,, ,, ,,	
1588 Nov. 10	Richard s ,, Denton ,,	

160⁰₁ Feb. 17   Hugh Rawodd Vicar of Ditchnige and
               Anne Warren alias Deane, mar.
1601 Dec. 13   Henry s Hugh Rawod Minister, bap.
1603 June 28   Susan d Hugh Rawod Minister, bap.
1604 June 19   Hughe Rawod Vicar bur.
(1626 Apr. 8   Mrs. Anne Rawood widow, bur.)

NOTE.—His administration and her will are at Lewes.

Anthony Mattock, 1604-1606, was a cousin of Anthony Watson, Bishop of Chichester 1596-1605. Lower's " Sussex Worthies " informs us that the Bishop, who died and was buried at Cheam, where he had formerly been Rector, left the residue of his library (after special bequests of books to other persons) to his cousins, who were John Mattock (the Archdeacon), William Mattock, and Anthony Mattock, Vicar of Ditchling.

Anthony Mattock was afterwards Rector of Rodmell and West Firle; he died about 1620.

The history of an amusing quarrel which took place in the parish in the year 1607, between two ladies, may now be related.

The parties engaged in the dispute, which seems to have been a fierce one, were Mrs. Rawood, the widow of the late, and Mrs. Price, the wife of the then Vicar of the parish. It seems that the widow was loth to give up possession of the pew in the church which she had occupied during her husband's ministry; Mrs. Price being as determined that she should give it up, thus the warfare began, and was kept up for some time with much spirit on either side. At last the matter was reported to the Ordinary, and by him referred to the Archdeacon and another judge of the Ecclesiastical Court at Lewes, and by them remitted to a sort of Parish Court at Ditchling, in the following manner:—

" To our very lovinge ffriends the Church Wardens,

sidesmen and parishioners of Ditchling, Salutem in Christo"

After stating the question in dispute, "they are directed to take three or four substantial men of the parish to their counsel to determine the matter."

The decision of this Parish Court was given against the widow, but how little she heeded it, is shown in the conclusion of their report, which says:—

"We will justifie at all times, upon our oathes if need be, that, in this action, we have done no wrong, neither to Mrs. Rawoode, nor her daughter Anne Warren, for three incumbents wives did sitt in the same seate before; and thus we have determined of this matter according to the authoritie given and directed unto us, truely and faithfullye without partialitye, as in conscience we thought fit, and yet notwithstanding the saide Anne Warren by her mother's advise, contrary to your ecclesiastical authoritie and our order and determination still molesteth the saide Mrs. Price and, after a violent manner keepeth the sayde pew, contrary to all right and conscience; and thus humbly desiring that the sayde Mrs. Rawoode and her daughter Anne may be sharply censured for the manifest contempt given to your authoritie, and the breach of your order in this matter, and for the publike evil example given to the whole congregation and thus we humbly take our leaves and commend you to God.

"Nov. 4th, Anno Dom. 1607."

This document was signed by two churchwardens, two sidesmen, and twenty-one of the inhabitants.

A subsequent entry in the churchwardens' accounts, in which the foregoing information is to be found, states that "a seat was built up in the prebends chancel, at the right hand going out of the body of the church, being designedly built for the vicar's wife."

Thus there is every reason to think that, in spite of the decision of the Parish Court and "the publike evil example given to the whole congregation," the widow and her daughter bid them all defiance and triumphed, and not only so, but we find that Mrs. Rawood outlived Mrs. Price some five years and saw her old antagonist Mrs. Price become Mrs. Pritchett.

1609 May 29 John s Thomas Price Clearke bap.
  „   June 14 John Price s Thomas Price bur.
1621 Aug. 20 Mr. Thomas Price ye Vicar of this parish bur.
162½ Feb. 11 Thomas Pritchett and Elizabeth Price widow married.

NOTE.—The will of Thomas Price is at Lewes.

1625 Nov. 3 Thomas Price s Mr. Thomas Price bur.

Mascall Giles (the next vicar) was a cousin of John Mascall, of Plumpton (who mentions him as such, in his will, proved 27th March, 1641, at Lewes), and married there on 13th February, 162½, Sarah Higginbotham. The following extracts from the Ditchling registers refer to them and their family.

Baptisms.		Burials.
1622 Nov. 10	John s Mascall Giles, Clerk and Sarah	163¾ Feb. 24
1624 Mar. 25	Eleanor d Mascall Giles Clerk	1626 Aug. 27
1627 Aug. 19	Henry s Mascall Giles Clerk	1627 Oct. 20
1628 Oct. 5	Eleanor d Mascall Giles...	
163$^0_1$ Feb. 27	Edward s Mascall Giles Clerk	
1633 May 20	Samuel s Mascall Giles Vicar	
1635 Oct. 14	Thomas s Mascall Giles ...	1639 Sep. 7
163⅞ Feb. 25	Nathaniel s Mascall Giles Clerk	1639 July 17
1640 May 19	Mary d Mascall Giles Minister	
	Sarah wife of Mascall Giles	1640 Sep. 5
164$^0_1$ Feb. 26	Mascall Gyles Minister and Francis Browne wid (mar).	

Mascall Giles, in 1635, contributed 5s. to repairing St. Paul's Church, in London. His writing in the Ditchling Registers ends 4th April, 1644, but we believe the Burrell MSS. in the British Museum state that he was still Vicar in 1650.

An order of the Committee of Plundered Ministers on February 2nd, 1647-8, refers to "Mr. John Buckley, late Minister of Ditchling," and another order on the same day states that "Mr. Buckley the former minister thereof hath sithence left the said church and that one Mr. Snell a godlie and orthodox divine, is settled there" (Bodleian MS., No. 325, p. 233).

1648 Apr. 11.—Thomas s Samuel and Susan Snell bap.

1650 Apr. 21.—Samuel s Samuel and Susan Snell bap.

Although Sir William Burrell gives the name of Nicholas White as an incumbent during the Commonwealth, he was in reality only the maltster or husbandman who was chosen by the inhabitants on the 20th September, 1653, to keep the register book, and approved of by Henry Shelley, Esq., J.P., on the 30th of November in the same year.

The Presbyterian minister who probably succeeded Mr. Snell was Edward Lulham, and the following entries from the registers give the baptisms of his children:

1652 Apr. 7.—Sarah d Edward Lulham bap.

165¾ March 20.—Mary d Edward Lulham bap.

1658 Oct. 18.—Edward s Edward Lulham bap.

and the following is probably the burial of one of the daughters:—

167¾ Jan. 13.—Mary d Mr. Lulham bur.

Edward Lulham was ejected in 1662, in which year a baptism, marriage, and burial are recorded " by me John Gravett, Vicar," the earliest, the marriage, being on the 28th September in that year. His tenure of the Vicarage and that of his successor were both short, as on the 15th August, 1664, John Crumpe, M.A., was admitted, and the burial of Mr. John Crumpe, Vicar, is recorded in the registers under the date of 24th April, 1666.

The following is the baptismal entry of the son of the vicar who succeeded Mr. Crump:—

1670 Apr. 10.—Edward son of William Willys Vicar and of Rebecca his wife, baptized.

John Parker, admitted on the death of William Willys, was also Rector of Clayton, where he was buried. He died on the 28th December, 1691, aged 49.

His place of sepulture is marked by a black marble slab in the nave of Clayton Church, near the chancel.

1692 July 30.—John Nicholls admitted on the death of John Parker was Curate of Ditchling in October, 1678, when (and subsequently) he signs as such several entries of burials in woollen.

1688. "Mary the wife of Thos. Dancy was buried on the 12th of May and no affidavit made and brought to be recorded that she was buried in woollen according to act of Parliament for burying in woollen and on the 19th I John Nicholls sent out my information thereof to Thos. Beard of Hurstpierpoint Esq. one of His Majesty's Justices of the Peace delivering it to Nicholas Marchant one of the Church wardens to deliver to the aforesaid Thos. Beard and he ordered Thos Dancy to pay 50s. into the hands of the overseers of Ditchling to disburse to the poor thereof."

The Act for burying in woollen was passed in 1678, and the relatives of deceased persons were required to make oath that the corpse was not " put in, wrapt or wound up, or buried in any shirt, sheet, or shroud made or mingled with flax, hemp, silk or hair, gold or silver, or other than what is made of sheep's wool, nor in any coffin, lined or cased with any cloth stuff or any other thing whatsoever made or mingled with the aforesaid materials but sheeps wool only."

The Dan:ys connected with Ditchling for many generations seem to have been publicans, for a " Catalogue of Taverns in tenne Shires about London," by John Taylor, London, 1636, mentions " At Ditchelling James Dansey."

1691 Dec. 19.—Dorothy wife of John Nichols buried in flannel.

1715.—Mr. John Nichols Vicar Dyed ye 20th buried Aprill ye —— Affidavit made the 24th (i.e., that he was buried in woollen).

Elnathan Iver, inducted August 10th, 1715, was in 1718 also presented to the Vicarage of Wivelsfield, and he continued to hold the two livings until his death in 1721. In his will dated 19th June, 1721, and proved at Lewes 25th October, 1721, he desires to be buried on the north-west side of the churchyard of Ditchling, " in the outbounds in the rock with as little company and charge and as privately as conveniently can be." He also mentions his sisters, Elizabeth Whithe, Mrs. Anne, and Mrs. Joan Bickerton, and his cousin, Mary May.

The memorial tablet to his memory may be seen outside the west door of the church on the right hand side; the inscription, in Latin, is as follows:—

" Hic jacet corpus Elnathan Iver cujus Animae propitius fit Deus per Jesum Christum Dominum nostrum. In quo pacifico spes mea sola manet. Obit 30 Die July Anno Domini 1721. Ætatis Suæ 66."

The registers, however, give a different date for his death, viz.:

1721 Oct. 2.—Elnathan Iver (bur.).

There is, therefore, evidently a mistake either on the tombstone or in the registers.

1721 Dec. 11.—William Lamb, admitted on the death of Elnathan Iver, also held the living of Wivelsfield from 1731 to 1739, and in 1726 gave £200 as an augmentation to the living of Ditchling. The following entries are from the register of baptisms:—

1722 Sep. 21. Sarah d Wm. and Eliz. Lamb.
1723 Oct. 4. Eliz. d Wm. and Eliz. Lamb.
172⁴⁄₅ Mar. 22. Mary d Wm. and Eliz. Lamb.
172⁶⁄₇ Feb. 21. John Taylor s Wm. and Eliz. Lamb ⎫
172⁶⁄₇ Feb. 21. Springett s Wm. and Eliz. Lamb ⎬ ? Twins

On the 29th September, 1740, "Edwd. Powel Vicar," signs his name in the 3rd volume of the Ditchling Registers. Extract from Registers:

1746 The Reverend Mr. Edward Powell Vicar of this Parish was buryed May 16th.

A slab in front of the pulpit records:—

"Here Lyeth Interrd ye body of the Revd Mr. Edward Powel late Vicar of this Parish who Departed this life the 13th day of May 1746 aged 33 years."

His will was proved at Lewes in 1749, and therein he mentions his father, Edward, his brothers, William and John, his sister, Elizabeth Powell, and his wife, Jane. Extract:—

1783 Mrs. Jane Powell from Wivelsfield AET 83 (bur.) Dec. 29.

(Mr. Powell also held the living of Wivelsfield.)

Daniel Walter, admitted June 3rd, 1746, was probably the son of the Vicar of Cuckfield of the same name, who married a daughter of Thomas Manningham (Bishop of Chichester 1709-1722), and to whom there is a memorial in Cuckfield Church.

Samuel Jefferies, admitted 3rd March, 1746-7, signs the 3rd vol. of Registers as Vicar, 25th March, 1747. From Registers:—

1777 The Rev. Mr. Jefferies Vicar of Ditchling buried March 7.

NOTE.—Mr. Jefferies was also Rector of Patcham.

An altar tomb situated to the north-west of the church records that:—

"Beneath this tomb are deposited the remains of the Rev. Saml. Jefferies who was Vicar of this Parish, he died March 2nd 1777 AET 63.

"Also the remains of Mrs. Ann Jefferies his widow who departed this life March 4th 1786 aged 71 years."

Passing over the name of Joseph Bailey, 1777-1794, who seems to have succeeded to the Rectory of Patcham as well as the Vicarage of Ditchling, we find that his successor, John Hanley, appears to have been Vicar of Wivelsfield from 1787-1789. He held Ditchling for about nine months only, and was succeeded by Thomas Hudson, 1795-1820, who was also Vicar of Wivelsfield, 1796-1802. There was a Vicar of Brighton of the same name, 1789 to 1804, in which year he resigned that living to become Rector of Fittleworth. Horsfield's "History of Sussex," Vol i., 145, says:—

"Thomas Hudson who resigned the Vicarage of Brighton 1804 became Rector of Fittleworth and was Vicar of Ditchling."

The obituary notice which appeared in the "Gentleman's Magazine" at the date of his death was a follows:—

"May 12th, 1819.—At the Parsonage Fittleworth near Petworth Sussex aged 69, the Rev. Thomas Hudson M.A. of St. John's College Cambridge, formerly Vicar of Brighton, Chaplain to His Royal Highness the Prince Regent and a Prebendary of Chichester Cathedral, but latterly for many years Vicar of Fittleworth in the same diocese."

It seems almost certain that the Vicar of Ditchling and Rector of Fittleworth were one and the same person. It will be noticed also that the Rev. Denny Ashburnham succeeded the year following Mr. Hudson's death, who probably kept a curate in charge at Ditchling.

The fact may be noted, in passing, that Mr. Hudson was the builder and owner of the Chapel Royal, North Street, Brighton.

Denny Ashburnham, 1820-1843, was of the same

family as the Right Rev. Sir William Ashburnham, Bart., who was Bishop of Chichester 1754-1797. It is interesting to note that the first baronet was Sir Denny Ashburnham, of Broomhall Park, Guestling, who received his title in 1660 on the restoration of Charles II. The Ashburnhams were ever staunch adherents of the Stuarts, even when the fortunes of that luckless Royal Family were at the lowest ebb.

Denny Ashburnham also held the living of Catsfield, near Hastings, and during the latter part of his vicariate Ditchling was in charge of a curate, the Rev. John George Ash, a gentleman much respected, and who subsequently became Vicar of Lodsworth, in West Sussex.

By his wife, Caroline Selby, the Rev. John George Ash had two children, baptised at Ditchling as follows:

Jane Maria Marrian 24th Nov. 1833.

Selby Attree Horne 21st May 1837.

The latter was a godson of Thomas Attree, of Queen's Park, Brighton.

Another gentleman, who held the position of curate-in-charge during Denny Ashburnham's vicariate, was Henry James, who in 1843 became Vicar of Willingdon, and it was some seven years later that he met his death in a very sudden and tragic manner.

The facts are painfully simple.

While out one day walking on the cliffs, near Beachy Head, in company with his little daughter and a friend, it appears that Mr. James, probably for the purpose of obtaining a better view of some object in the distance, ventured too near the edge of the cliffs, when, without any warning, the treacherous ground gave way beneath him, and he was dashed to the shore below and killed.

Julius Nouaille (a French refugee name) is buried at Ditchling, where a tomb situated to the north-west of the church bears this inscription:—

" Beneath this tombstone are deposited the remains

of the Rev. Julius Nouaille B.A. Eleven years vicar of this parish who departed this life Feb. 2nd. 1855, aged 49 years."

The extensive restorations carried out during the incumbency of the Rev. Thos. Hutchinson have already been noted. He held the living for nearly thirty years, and the memorials to his memory include a stained glass window in the chancel, the cost of which was defrayed by the parishioners. It bears the following inscription:—

"To the Glory of God and in loving memory of Thomas Hutchinson Priest, for twenty eight years Vicar of this Parish who fell asleep November 13th A.D. 1883 aged 80."

The window, though small, is a beautiful one, and depicts the incident of the Saviour healing the blind man, and the words " Jesus said unto him Receive thy sight," also appear.

For a considerable time before his decease Mr. Hutchinson had been prevented, through infirmity, from active ministry in the church, and the duties were in charge of a curate.

Mr. Hutchinson was laid to rest in a tomb beneath the shadow of the church in which he had ministered for so many years and had loved so well; his grave will be found hard by the belfry entrance.

His widow, who survived him fourteen years, died in the autumn of 1896, at Leamington, where for some years she had resided, and was brought to Ditchling to be buried in the same grave with her husband.

At this funeral occurred an incident which must surely be unique, and therefore we chronicle it.

It seems that funerals took place at Newtimber and at Ditchling almost at the same time, and it was a strange coincidence that in the case of both, the coffins came by rail to Hassocks; that for Newtimber arrived by a certain train, and started for its destination.

Shortly after this a second train arrived conveying

the coffin for Ditchling. Following this came a telegram notifying the Hassocks officials that two gentlemen having missed the train, were coming down by a special to attend the "funeral." In due course they arrived, were conducted to a mourning coach which had been delayed to await their coming, and were driven off to Ditchling to attend, as the sequel proved, the wrong funeral.

The strange mistake was not discovered until the ceremony was half concluded, and though the journey was then made to Newtimber, they were of course too late to take part in the service there.

The present Vicar of Ditchling is the Rev. Francis Collins Norton, of University College, Durham, to whom the writer has much pleasure in dedicating this little work.

CHAPTER VIII.

MONUMENTAL INSCRIPTIONS AND MEMORIALS.

THERE are no memorials to the Michelbournes in Ditchling Church, though we believe members of that family found their last resting place in the chancel.

In former years it would seem to have been a matter of little moment to destroy memorials of the dead. Ditchling has been no exception. The slabs which should commemorate the Michelbournes have probably been ruthlessly torn up and cast away during a perhaps too diligent "restoration."

This was evidently the fate of that marking the burial place of Dr. James Hougham, which, in records of the church before restoration, is described as being "a slab near communion table," and reading thus:—

"Here lyeth the body of Dr. James Hougham who dyed the 2nd November 1700. Also here lyeth Mary his wife who dyed the 5th of October 1688, being of the ancient family of the Culpeppers."

The Culpeppers built Wakehurst Place, Ardingly; they were an important family in Sussex. Why Dr. Hougham and his wife were buried in the chancel we do not know, unless he was a relative of the Turners, as all the other memorials are to that family. There is, however, a record of a Turner leasing a house in Ditchling to a Dr. Hougham for a number of years.

The Turner memorials are all stone slabs in the chancel pavement, except the first, which is a beautiful piece of Sussex marble, and reads thus:—

I.

"Here lyeth buryed the body of Thomas Turner late of Kymer, aged four skore and four years, who departed this life the aythe day of February in the year of our Lord 1671."

This was the gentleman who had purchased the tithes of Ditchling. The reader will note the spelling on his tomb gives the correct pronunciation of the word Keymer, also a very peculiar and original method of spelling the word eighth.

II.

"Here lyeth buried the body of Richard Turner, late of Oldland in Keymer, who was the son of Thomas Turner, being aged sixty foure yeeres and departed this life July the first Anno Dom. 1681."

III.

"Here is interred the body of Richard Turner, gent late of Oldland in Keymer, who departed this life October the 2nd. Anno Domini 1720 Aetatis suae 68."

IV.

"Here lieth the body of Richard Turner of Oldland gent, eldest son of Richard and Sarah his wife, who departed this life the 14th of Maye 1748 aged 59. Under the old stone South of this lieth the body of Jane, wife ot Richard Turner of Oldland Gent, youngest daughter of Thomas and Amy Gratwick of Ham in Angmering, who departed this life Sept 21st 1728 aged 37 and left Issue, Richard, William, Thomas and Amy."

V.

"Here lieth the body of William Turner; Apothecary and Citizen, who departed this life October 11th 1733 Aged 33; and left no Issue."

VI.

"Here lies the body of Thomas Turner, youngest son of Richard and Jane his wife, who departed this life the 26th of February 1745 aged 21."

VII.

"Here lies the body of Richard Turner of Oldland gent eldest son of Richard and Jane his wife who departed this life the 17th of April 1754 aged 36."

VIII.

"In memory of William Turner of Oldland in the parish of Keymer Gent, who died the 26th daye of June 1786 aged 65 years. He was the last surviving son of Richard and Jane Turner, whose remains are deposited in this chancel. And also of Mrs. Sarah Turner, the relict of the above named William Turner, and daughter of the late Rev. Edward Wilson rector of Westmeston, she departed this life the 3rd day of May 1802 aged 77 years."

IX.

"To the memory of the five children of William and Sarah Turner viz. :—

"Mary Jane, a resident of this Parish born Jan. 7th 1757, died Sept. 14th 1857 and was buried in the churchyard (age 100 years and 8 months).

"Thomas late of Oldland in Keymer to which he succeeded at his father's death, born August the 28th 1759 died March the 4th 1827 and was buried in the churchyard of that Parish (age 67½ years).

"Sarah Frances, who married first John Attree of this Parish and secondly Thomas Thompson of London. Born May the 18th 1761 died at Timworth in Suffolk Feb: 21st 1856 and was buried in the churchyard of that Parish (age 94 years and 3 months).

"Richard in Holy Orders Rector of Grately in Hampshire Born May 13th 1763, died at Lambeth Oct: 17th 1819, and was buried in the new burial ground of that Parish.

"Elizabeth Anne also a resident of this Parish Born June 8th 1766 died Sept. 17th 1850 and was buried in the churchyard in the same grave as her sister Mary Jane (age 84 years and 3 months)."

With the following memorial, which is in the churchyard, we will conclude those to the Turner family.

X.

"In loving memory of Mary Jane, Third daughter of Thomas Turner, Born at Oldland Keymer Jan 8th 1803 died at Ditchling March 19th 1886 (age 83 yrs and 2 months)."

For a very full and interesting pedigree of the family of Turner, of Oldland and Ditchling, the reader is referred to Vol xxv., Sussex Arch. Coll.

In the south chancel was formerly a slab with the following inscription in capitals:—

> (PETER) MARCHANT
> OF DICHLAND DISE
> ASED MAYE THE
> FIRST 1661.

and from the Register of Burials, 1661, "Petter Marchant singor," 3rd May.

From his will at Lewes, we learn that he had a wife Mary, sons Peter and Richard, minors, daughters Elizabeth, Mary, Ann, and Sarah, and brothers Richard and Thomas.

We have before noted that the Marchants were connected with the family of Turner, and that probably accounts for some of the family being interred here, though we have no trace of any further memorials to them. Another memorial, also in the south chancel and in capitals, but nearly obliterated and worn away, yet identical with an entry in the parish registers, is the following:—

> 1598.
> HERE LIETH CONSTANCE
> HAUSE WIDOW WHO
> DIED THE 3 OF JAN.

From her will at Lewes, Mrs. Hawes appears to have been a sister of Thomas Rootes, then of Ditchling, and of Eleanor, wife of Richard Hider, of Ditchling, and to have been the second wife and widow of John Hawes, who was buried at Salehurst.

The family entered their pedigree at the Visitation of Sussex in 1662.

The following are also in the south chancel:—

"To the memory of Ann wife of Jas Wood of this parish who departed this life the 29th of September 1776 aged 76 years."

"To the memory of James Wood late of this parish who departed this life the 2nd June 1790 aged 90 years. Also of Mary, daughter of James Wood and Ann his wife, who departed this life the 8th January 1736 aged 1 year and 11 months."

This James Wood was probably the churchwarden whose name appears on No. 5 bell.

Ann, wife of James Wood, was daughter of Robert Chatfield, of Handly, in Cuckfield, where she was baptised 3rd March, 1700, and was married at Wivelsfield 10th April, 1726. Her grandfather was Robert Chatfield, who migrated from Ditchling to Cuckfield.

Also near to the above is the following:—

"In memory of Arthur Deudney, Second son of Arthur and Sarah Deudney who died Janry 14th 1816 aged 7 years."

A slab in the south transept bears this inscription:—

"In memory of Mrs. Sarah Price, relict of Mr. Nathaniel Price late of Bermondsey, Southwark, who died December 29th 1794 aged 75 years."

In the south chancel are two ancient slabs which have been despoiled of their brasses; one evidently having borne the effigies of a man and woman, with a legend at their feet, and the other a simple epitaph plate. It is not unlikely that these brasses marked the burial place of members of the Michelbourne family. There are also three monumental slabs of 12th and 13th century fixed upright against the wall in the porch. These were originally in the chancel. There is no trace of an inscription on any of them, but they are rather

THE POOLE MONUMENT.

elaborate in design, though at the present time much mutilated. The general belief seems to be that they were the memorials of former vicars.

The most ancient memorial in the church, and certainly one of the most interesting, is that in the north transept, described as "a mural half table monument," having this inscription along the frieze in capital letters:—

"Here lyeth Henry Poole Esquier, who dyed the 28th daye of Marche Ao. Dni. 1580."

The monument is divided by short pillars of Grecian architecture and stylobates into four niches, three of which contain shields bearing coats of arms, now much mutilated, and having at some destructive period been covered with a thick coating of whitewash, utterly destroying the heraldic colours with which no doubt they were originally emblazoned.

We cannot do better than quote from the description which Lieutenant, now Lieut.-Colonel F. W. T. Attree, R.E., F.S.A., gives of this monument in Vol. xxviii., Sussex Archæological Collections, which says:—

"The tinctures are here inserted from pedigrees and other heraldic works."

I.—In the first niche is a shield of arms, with the following quarterings:—

1st and 4th a lion rampant between eight fleur de lys (Poole)

2nd and 3rd a Chevron between three stags heads cabossed (Bruerton of co. Cheshire).

The crest, which is very much damaged, is probably "out of a ducal coronet or, a griffin's head ar."

II.—On a shield this achievement of Arms for Margaret, daughter of George, 3rd Lord Abergavenny, and wife of the above Henry Poole.

1. Gu., on a saltire arg., a rose of the field barbed and seeded proper (Neville of Raby).
2. Or, fretty gu, on a canton per pale erm, and or, a galley sa (Neville of Bulmer).

3. Gu., a fesse between six cross crosslets or, (Beauchamp).
4. Barry of ten (? Boteville alias Thynne).
5. A lion rampant (probably Boteville).
6. Chequee or and az., a chevron erm., (Newburgh) but the chevron is missing.
7. Quarterly arg., and gu., in the 2nd and 3rd quarters a frette or, over all a bend sa. (Le Despensers).
8. Gu., three chevronels or, (De Clare).

III.—The shield from this niche has been taken away.

IV.—As in I., but the crest is gone.

Henry Poole was descended from Thomas Poole, of Poole in Cheshire, through John Poole, his second son, who was servant to the Lady Abbess of Wilton, and whose son Richard settled at Sapperton in Gloucester, where his grandson Henry was born.

The following is an extract from the will of Henry Poole, of Dycheling Esquire, dated 28th January, 1580. He directs that his body "is to be buried in the church of Dycheling behynde my pewe there in the Northsyde of the saide church," and that a decent tomb of stone with his arms and name to be engraved thereupon be erected; he gives ten pounds to the poor of Ditchling and five pounds to the poor of Keymer, to be paid within one year after his death. He bequeaths to his sons John and Francis Poole the whole of his farm and grounds of Shortfurth and Frinckeborowe, mentions Lawrence Newton and William Apsley, Esq., his godson Henry Beach, Thomas Beach of Keymer, Thomas Button of Wivelsfield, and Thomas Wilson, who is to enjoy his moitie of Frynckeborowe. He mentions Margaret his wife and George his son, "joint taken with my wife of the Park of Dycheling and the farm of Keymer." He mentions his property in Blackfriars, London, and his land in Co. Somerset. To his brother Sir Giles Poole, Knt., he leaves his best nag, mentions his nephew Henry, the son of the said Sir Giles, also his cousin Henry Poole and Sycelye Fetyplace.

He also mentions his son Thomas Poole and grandson Charles Poole, under age.

To his good Lord Rt. Honourable Henry Lord Abergavenny he leaves his best armour and best steel saddle, mentions his two sons Henry and William Poole, and makes Sir John Pelham Knt. and John Shurley Esq. surveyors of his will.

The place which the monument now occupies is not quite the position assigned to it in the will. It formerly stood against the wall under the west window of the north transept, whence it was removed to its present position against the north wall when the church was restored; we are thus able to locate Henry Poole's pew in Ditchling Church. It was, of course, in this north transept, which was probably divided from the other part of the church by an oak screen; the stone piers which carry the transept arch reveal traces of having been mended after the removal of the holdfasts, by which the screen was doubtless fixed to them.

We have already given the inscription on the slab in front of the pulpit to the memory of Edward Powell (Vicar), and we now propose to give the modern memorials.

The east end of the chancel is panelled in oak up to the string course, the upper portion consisting of ornamental Gothic arching, with more elaborate work immediately behind the altar. The centre panel bears a shield with the sacred monogram.

An interesting fact, in connection with this beautifully executed piece of work, is that it was designed, built, and carved by two brothers, natives of Ditchling. It has the following inscription on a brass plate:—

"This panelling was erected to the Glory of God and in revered and loved memory of John Botting Tuppen and Jane his wife, also of Alfred Chassereau and Henry their beloved sons.

"Easter, 1892."

The west window of stained glass, beautiful in colours and workmanship, represents the adoration of the Magi, and is inscribed "In Memoriam Henry et Rebecca Tuppen," and beneath is a brass plate recording—

"To the memory of Henry Tuppen and Rebecca his wife late of Brighton, Henry deceased Janry. 22 1852 Rebecca deceased Feb. 22 1856."

The three decorated windows of the nave are filled with stained glass representing "The Garden of Gethsemane," "The Crucifixion," and "The Descent from the Cross," "The Ascension," etc., and are inscribed respectively "Frances Elizae Attree," "Thomas Attree," "W. Wakeford Attree."

Having concluded our notes on the memorials in the church, which we have given in full, we will turn to those in the churchyard. These we purpose to treat in a somewhat different manner, as it would not be possible to give each inscription. A copy of the inscriptions taken in 1877 by Lieutenant F. W. T. Attree is to be seen in the library of the Sussex Archæological Society at Lewes, and a copy of this MS. is in possession of the Vicar.

There are about forty inscriptions to the Attree family, who have been connected with this neighbourhood for nearly five hundred years, being descended from John Atte Ree, Lord of the Manor of Otehall in Wivelsfield, whose grandson William At Ree had two sons, viz., Thomas, Lord of the Manor of Otehall, which passed to the family of Godman by marriage of his daughter and heiress with Walter Godman about 1527; and Richard Att Ree, of Theobalds in Wivelsfield, who died shortly before the 18th September, 1526. This property descended from father to youngest son until 1765, when on the death of Thomas Attree it went to his sister Dorothy, wife of John Mill of Westmeston, and by marriage with her daughter Dorothy (his first wife, by whom he had no issue) to John Attree, of Ditchling, whose son of the same name, by Sarah Frances Turner, his second wife, sold Theobalds in 1823.

The following coat of arms is borne by this family: Per chevron or and vert, in chief two oak trees eradicated proper, and in base, a cinquefoil of the first. For a short pedigree of the family see Appendices.

The earliest tomb to the name in Ditchling Churchyard is a double headstone inscribed:—

"In memory of Elizabeth wife of William Attree who departed this life Janry 1st. 1741 aged 59 years. In memory of William Attree late of this parish who departed this life July the first 1747 aged 67 years."

It would be out of the question to notice every inscription to this family. The tombs occupy a considerable portion of the churchyard, and all the memorials are in good preservation and readable, but we purpose giving a few facts relating to the history of this family.

The grandson of the above-mentioned William Attree is described as "William Attree of Brighton, Gent, obit August 1810 aet 63 years." This gentleman was a solicitor in that town, and his two sons also held leading positions among the principal inhabitants in Brighton. The elder of the two, Thomas Attree, was solicitor to the Royal Family, he was Lord of the Manor of Atlingworth, which embraces a considerable part of Brighton, and there he enclosed many acres of delightfully wooded and undulating land, and formed a beautiful park and built a large mansion. Mr. Attree obtained permission from Queen Adelaide, the Consort of William IV., to call his park "Queen's Park," the name which it bears to this day. The idea, however, that it was built for Queen Adelaide (as some have supposed), or that she retired there after the death of her Royal husband, is without foundation. There are few of the inhabitants of Brighton now living who can recall the Queen's Park of Mr. Attree's day.

The mansion, which is still standing at the north-west end of the park, was designed by Barry. The private gardens surrounding it were laid out in the Italian style from the plans of the same architect, and are said to have been very beautiful and to have cost an enormous expenditure.

After the death of Mr. Attree, the park passed into the possession of those who cared not, or perhaps could not maintain it as it had been, and gradually the gardens became neglected, and the pleasantly-wooded slopes and valleys a dreary waste. Those of us who can remember it at this time, and till within very recent years, and who perchance passed that way and obtained an occasional glimpse through an open gate or a rent in the wall, will recall a lonely and desolate wilderness of overgrown trees and long grass, giving little evidence of former beauty. But another change was to take place, and in time a considerable portion was sold for building purposes; and yet another change, the nucleus was presented to the inhabitants of Brighton for ever. When this came to pass the Corporation lost no time in converting it into a once more pleasant spot, and now the valley, one of the prettiest in the neighbourhood of Brighton, with its nicely kept walks and flower beds, its miniature waterfall and ornamental water, seems to have regained something of what it once was, though the area which the park now covers is considerably smaller than it was formerly.

Mr. Attree found a last resting place amongst his ancestors in Ditchling Churchyard, where a memorial to his memory and to that of his only son (who predeceased him) reads as follows:—

" Thomas Attree of Queen's Park Brighton died February VIIth, MD.CCCLXIII in the LXXXVIth year of his age having survived W. Wakeford Attree his only

THE CHURCH IN 1780.

son one year and eleven days. William Wakeford Attree M.A. Recorder of Rye Hastings and Seaford, died January XXVIIIth. MD.CCCLXII aged LVI years."

The three stained glass windows in the north wall of the nave are also to the memory of the Attrees of Queen's Park.

The following is the memorial to Mr. Attree's brother:—

"Sacred to the memory of William Attree Esqre R.H.A., F.R.C.S., Surgeon Extraordinary to their late Majesties George IVth and William IVth, died 22nd April 1846 at Sudbury Grove in the County of Middlesex aged 67 years."

There are inscriptions to several sons of the above-named William Attree. The eldest, Francis Town Attree, B.A., was incumbent of Middleton, Derbyshire, and died at Bognor, 1858, aged 44. The second son, William Hooper Attree, Esq., M.R.C.S., is described as surgeon to His late Highness Don Miguel de Braganza, ex-King of Portugal, was warden of Sackville College, East Grinstead, and died in 1875, aged 58 years. Another son, Alfred Mackinnon Attree, Esq., Barrister-at-Law, for 23 years of the Tithe and Enclosure Commission, died in 1863, aged 38 years. Captain Frederick Simes Attree, H.M. 31st Regiment, was the youngest son, and was killed before Sebastopol on the 8th September, 1855, aged 27, and was buried in the presence of the whole regiment on Cathcarts Hill, where a stone to mark the spot and to record his upright name has been erected by his colonel and brother officers.

On the north side of the churchyard is a headstone:

"In memory of Nicholas Chaloner and his sister Sarah Chaloner, inhabitants of this Parish. They departed this life he the 1st of Nov. 1797 aged 92 years, she the 11th November 1796 aged 87. They were the son and daughter of Nicholas Chaloner formerly of

Stantons, Gent and Elizabeth his wife whose remains were interred and to their memory a stone was erected in the Churchyard of Plumpton."

This family, one of the oldest in Sussex, but long since fallen into decay, bore for their arms az : a chevron arg between three mascles or. Stantons, their home in Chiltington, is now a farmhouse, and was sold in 1714 by the above Nicholas Chaloner and Elizabeth his wife to Michael Marten. The Manor of Stantons consisted of one messuage, one shop, two gardens, two orchards, 60 acres of land, 20 acres of meadow, 50 acres of pasture, 10 acres of wood, and 10 acres of furze and heath, with appurtenances in Westmeston, Chiltington, and Chailey. About the year 1797 Stantons passed from the Martens to the family of John Marten Cripps.

Records of the family of Chaloner are preserved in the Parish Registers of Chailey, Chiltington, and Plumpton.

There are several members of the family of Scrase buried on the north side of the churchyard, the earliest memorial dated 1770 and the latest 1874.

The family, which resided at Court Farm, were a branch of the Hangleton Scrases.

Another notable family long connected with Ditchling and Wivelsfield, and still represented in the neighbourhood, though not in Ditchling, is that of Tanner, to whom there are numerous memorials ; on one of which the family is described as of " East End in this Parish." Their monuments are near the west and south doors.

An altar tomb north of the church is " To the memory of John Saxby late of Laughton in this county Gent who died 2nd Sep. 1787 aged 42." The widow of this gentleman seems to have married again, for there is a memorial recording :—

" In memory of Sukey the wife of John Bull and widow of Mr. Saxby of Laughton Place who departed this life 22nd Dec. 1802 most deeply lamented, aged 48 years."

Sukey was daughter of John Attree of Ditchling.

Near at hand also are the tombs of John Bull (son of the first-named John Bull by a previous wife, Sukey Saxby being his second), his widow and a daughter.

The son was an uncle of Charles Bull, a very rich solicitor of Bedford Row, whose death intestate on the 26th March, 1890, was the cause of a great pedigree case.

Close to the belfry doorway is a tomb bearing this inscription:—

"Here lyeth buryed the body of Robard Agate son of John Agate of Warnham who died the 4th March 1693."

In the following century the name of Agate appears with frequency amongst the records of the Dissenting Chapel in Ditchling.

On the south side of the church, where most of the oldest memorials are situated, and where formerly stood the old yew tree, are several altar tombs worthy of notice, especially as the inscriptions are all but obliterated. The record on one is, or was, as follows:—

"Here lyeth buried ye body of William Chatfield of Ditchling, youngest son of Robert Chatfield of Newick who departed this life Dec. 10th 1694 aged 76 years."

Two tombs which, from their proximity to the above, are probably those of other members of this family, are unreadable.

The arms of Chatfield were Ar, a griffin segreant, sa on a chief ppr, three escallops of the field. Crest, an heraldic antelope's head, erased or, armed and ducally gorged or.

In the reign of Charles I., John Chatfield, of Ditchling, declining the honour of knighthood, was fined £10, the usual sum demanded in those days as composition for knighthood. In later years the Chatfields seem to have been dissenters, and were connected with the chapel in this place for many years.

Another altar tomb on the south side is to Richard Webb, and is dated 1737, and on the same " Marten Richard Webb, late of Fanhouse in Weevilsfield, who departed this life November the 8th, 1748, aged 53 years."

Another tomb of the same class is to Ann Dwite, daughter of John and Mary Dwite, the date appearing to be 1756, and her age 63.

Ann Dwite, of Ditchling, by her will dated 25th February, 1756, and proved at Lewes 15th December, 1756, left £50 to repair and build the almshouse, and £50 to repair old pews and other ornaments in Ditchling Church.

Another interesting memorial, but on the north side of the church, is—

" In memory of Thomas Smith the Son of Samuel and Ann Smith and Great Grandson of Michael and Ann Marten late of New Close in Keymer died 7th Janry 1803, aged 20 years."

No doubt the above Michael Marten was identical with the one who had purchased Stantons of Nicholas Chaloner in 1714.

An interesting memorial is the following, which will be found on a wooden monument south of the church:

" George Howell Born at West Hoathly June 6th. 1754 died at Ditchling May 7th. 1855 Aged 100 years and 336 days."

The longevity of the inhabitants of Ditchling has long been quoted as a proof of the healthy locality in which they have lived, and the burial registers of former years furnish interesting figures in this respect. In the year 1857, out of 12 burials (exclusive of four infants) 11 were over sixty years of age, viz., three between 60 and 70, two between 70 and 80, four between 80 and 90, one between 90 and 100, and one above 100.

In the infants' classroom at the National School hangs a small engraving of the venerable old man whose memorial we have just given. It portrays him after he had attained his 100th year, dressed in a plain smock frock, and seated in a high-back arm-chair; printed at the foot of the picture is the information that he was " Shoemaker of Ditchling Sussex."

A flat oval stone fixed in the outside wall at the west end of the church seems to have had this inscription :—

" nere this place lyeth the body of Mary wife of John Fuller who departed this life Oct. — 1733." (The rest illegible).

There are memorials to the old family of Borrer of Rusper. It is interesting to note that a member of the family of Borrer of Ditchling was one of the chief players in a cricket club at Oakendene, near Cowfold, which flourished from 1790 to 1815.

Close by the north-east gate of the churchyard is the tomb of the Boddington family. The inscription is as follows :—

" Robert Boddington, Surgeon, died 15th June 1863 aged 69 years, also Louisa widow of the above died 24th Feb. 1868 aged 65 years.

" Also of Mary Anne Boddington only child of Robert and Louisa Boddington who died on the 17th day of Oct. 1896 aged 50 years."

Louisa Boddington was a daughter of John and Mary Borrer, of Roles Croft, Ditchling.

Another interesting memorial on a wooden monument is that

" In memory of Richard Dann 23 years governor of Ditchling Workhouse who died July 16th 1861 aged 68 years."

The Ditchling Workhouse formerly stood at the south corner of Lewes Road. It was pulled down about the year 1872.

CHAPTER IX.

THE DITCHLING MEETING HOUSE.

"THIS place is noted for dissenters of almost all denominations"—so wrote the Rev. Mr. Morgan in 1780, and a History of Ditchling would, therefore, be incomplete without some notice of the dissenting place of worship, surrounded by its own burial ground, situated in East End Lane, Ditchling, and which has a history extending over a period of at least two hundred years, and is probably one of the oldest, if not the oldest, of its kind in Sussex.

For the use of much valuable information relating to this subject we are indebted to Miss E. Kensett, of Horsham, from whose interesting articles, published in a paper called "The Inquirer" of July 21 and 28 and August 4th, 1894, we shall quote.

"An early date for the establishment of the Congregation in Ditchling may be fixed, as their representatives voted against Matthew Caffyn's exclusion from the General Baptist Assembly in 1693 or 1696. Ditchling would also seem to have been a sort of headquarters for the Baptists of Sussex in days gone by, and the place in fact seems to belong more to the past, than the present, for the records tell of members gathered from nearly all parts of Sussex and beyond its borders even, thus Streat, Kingston, Westmeston, Cyemar (Keymer), Whalebridge Common, Clayton, Wivelsfield, Hurstpierpoint, St. John's Common, Chayley, Chiltington, Falmer, Bolney, Brighton, Henfield, Kuckfield, Lindfield, Balkham, Newick, Opham (Offham), Lewes, Beddingham, Slough Green, Cowfold, Southover, Ardingly, Turner's Hill, Slaugham, Firle, Rottendean, Crawley, Charlwood, Ifel (Isfield or

THE MEETING-HOUSE,

Ifield ?), Godstone, Hurstmonceaux, Battle, East Grinstead, Waldron, Pulboro', Ashurst, Shipley, Horsham, Hitchingfield, Cranbrook, Sevenoaks, Walberton, Chiddingly, and Fletching, all these places are represented.

"Some of these, one would think, must simply have gone to Ditchling to be baptised and so have had their names enrolled on the list; the size of the chapel and the distance they must travel to get to it does not allow us to suppose they all attended every Lord's day."

"The chapel has a singularly open trust deed; and this may have facilitated the gradual progression of the congregation to their present standpoint: when the number of Trustees are reduced to five they are empowered and required to choose twelve more to act with them, the property to be applied to such charitable uses as such trustees for the time being shall think most proper."

It appears from his will, dated 24th February, 1734-5, proved at Lewes 5th March, 1736, that Robert Chatfield, of Street, was the founder of the Meeting House, for in it he makes the following bequest:—

"And whereas there is a house built belonging to me for the Baptist to Meeting and Land to bury their Dead in at Ditchling Town my will is that my son Robert Chatfield should make a good Title to the same to Thomas Backman Thomas Wood Stephen Agate and Michael Marten at Fregbarrow when they shall demand it, and if he should refuse he is to pay them £150."

The testator, who was the son of John and Susan Chatfield, of Ditchling, baptised there 21st March, 1675-6, married Sarah, daughter of Michael Marten, by whom he had two sons, Robert of Street, and Michael of Court Gardens, in Ditchling. He died on the 24th January, 1736, and his tomb, with another to the Martens, and head stones to John Caffin, 1731, aged 9 . . .

years and Bridget, wife of John Caffin, 1730, aged 84, are the earliest memorials in the burying ground, which contains several tombs of his descendants. Perhaps the most noteworthy tomb in this cemetery is that to the memory of Samuel Thompson, who died 1837, which contains a long exposition of his faith, founded on 1 Cor. viii. 5.

The earliest record commences:—

"A List of the Persons Received into Church Communion by Baptism and Laying on of hands or by Letters of Commendation from Churches of the same faith with us beginning from the time of the ordination of John Dancey, Michael Marten, Step. Agate."

The first three received on the 5th June, 1737, were George Leopard, Richard Foster, and Rose, wife of Daniel Lewrey; the next two Edward Doust of Balkham (Balcombe) and Richard Hider of Hurst on 26th June, 1737; followed on 4th September, 1737, by James Browne, son of Peter Browne, of Ditchling.

A Matthew Caffin from Horsham, the 80th on the list, was received 22nd July, 1744. On August 14th, 1774, the messengers were Mr. Danl. Dobel and Mr. John Brooman or Boarman, as he is afterwards called. William Evershed is messenger on 27th October, 1776, John Boarman again 7th June, 1778, and 14th May, 1780.

The names of Dancy, Marten, and Agate occur with frequency in the chapel records. A tablet inside the chapel records the death of Michael Marten in 1775; he no doubt was the owner of Stantons.

A memorial stone in the chapel yard records the death of John Dancy, 1800, and Mary Dancy, 1822; above the names are carved a skull and an open book.

Among the earlier ministers of the chapel was William Evershed, whose name occupies a prominent place among the records of early dissenters in Sussex.

He was born in 1717, and is believed to have been a native of Barcombe. In the manuscript "Life of

THE HISTORY OF DITCHLING.

William Evershed," written by John Jeffrey, appears the following extract:—

"He delivered his first sermon at Ditchling, when he was but nineteen years old (in 1736). His discourse displayed so much information, connection, and originality, that his friends were greatly surprised at the performance, he continued for some years, though still in the service of a farmer, to preach there and in the surrounding villages."

In 1742 he removed to Billingshurst, and gathered a congregation together and built a chapel there, but he continued to be a frequent visitor to Ditchling and Lewes, and exercised supervision of the Baptist Chapels in those places for some 38 years. Up to the time of his death he often preached in Ditchling. His decease seems to have occurred somewhat suddenly.

"On Saturday June 29, 1799, he left home for Lewes, where he on the following day preached twice and administered the Lord's Supper."

"On Monday he returned to Mrs. Brown's, Ditchling, where he was seized with a fever; on the following Saturday he bid his friends a calm and cheerful farewell, in the eighty second year of his age."

Formerly, viz., about the years 1753 to 1762, the Ditchling congregation had branches, and services were held at Lewes, Maresfield, Turner's Hill, and Cuckfield. Records of curious customs now obsolete as religious ceremonies frequently occur, as the following:—

"Pursuant to ye appointment of Last Church Meeting there was a Love Feast and washing of feet at Frag-barrough (now Frankbarrow), on May 22 1753 by 145 persons in all."

"1767 Agreed that those members of this society who are persuaded of the duty of washing feet have the free consent of the church to practise it as it was performed June 22 1767 at Mr. Thos. Pannatts By ninety persons."

A certain "Brother Simmonds" was appointed as minister in 1762, but it appears he was not a success, as in 1764 it is recorded that "this Church hath sett very unesey under the Hearing of Our Friend John Simmonds for Some time Past, and now we do Generally Agree and Conclude to Silance and not approve of him in the office of the Ministry, until it is approved in General by this Congregation."

It is surely a matter for little surprise that after this, Brother John Simmonds "did openly and freely chuse to joyn another Cumunion."

In 1772 Brother Isaac Mott was desired to officiate occasionally as an elder, and Brother James Walder and Josiah Dancy were also appointed as well as "Michael Marten of Furl." In 1773 "Friend Thomas Agate is unanimously chose by the People to officiate in the ministry at Ditchling Meeting and he excepts of it." "Jon Smith" was appointed in 1775, and in 1776 Josiah Dancy, James Walder, and Thomas Agate were again nominated.

Although seven deacons were nominated in 1782, the next year there was a "want of Deacons." In 1783 John Burgess was selected as Elder. In the same year it is recorded:

"Under the consideration of being destitute of any Elder by reason of which disadvantage the order and regularity of Church discipline cannot be so well preserved, we have nominated our friends Josiah Dancy and Thos. Agate to serve us in that office."

In 1784 "The church still approves of them," and in 1788 Josiah Dancy and James Drowley were nominated.

There is a tablet to the memory of Josiah Dancy, who died in 1802, on the outside wall of the chapel. Mr. Drowley is believed to have emigrated to America, as did John Burgess, whose personal history is dealt with in future pages. Mr. Billinghurst also emigrated.

We again quote Miss Kensett's "Historic Notes":—

"The Billinghursts and Agates seem to have been fairly substantial property holders in and about Ditchling and Chailey, as well as at Shipley; one of the former family, who emigrated, is noted in the list of members as 'now Mrs. Van Vorice, America,' and an American letter tells how 'she has married a fat Dutchman and lives genteel in New York.' These two families intermarried more than once, and some of the oldest altar tombs in the chapel yard are theirs. Their connection with the chapel must have ceased soon after the beginning of this century."

There is an altar tomb in the chapel yard to the memory of John Billinghurst, who died 19th Dec., 1791, aged 77; Abigail, his wife, who died 5th Oct., 1774, aged 63; and of Thomas Agate, husband of their daughter Ann, who (he) died 23rd July, 1787, aged 30 or 50 years.

In the minute book of the chapel is an entry relating to Dr. Charles Lloyd, who was once settled as General Baptist Minister at Ditchling. He is said to have been one of the most accurate classical scholars the Unitarians ever had.

After this follow the names of Messrs. Davies and Snellgrove in 1802, and Mr. Thomas Sadler as a lay preacher, and in 1803 Abraham Bennett took charge of and remained the pastor of the congregation for 15 years, and if such a term is allowable in connection with Unitarianism, it would seem he was a "very advanced" member of the community. In 1805, we are told, "he commenced to preach at Cuckfield in the morning and at Ditchling in the afternoon," but in 1808 he was "desired to preach twice a day at Ditchling and he consented on condition the same money was raised as he then received at both places, but it is doubtful if this was done." He was also for some years evening lecturer of the Unitarian Chapel, Brighton, and he resigned Ditchling in 1818, and took charge of a congregation at Poole, in Dorsetshire.

118   THE HISTORY OF DITCHLING.

During his ministry two free schools were established, one for boys and one for girls, in East End Lane, Ditchling, and we will quote the following extract from " Horsfield's History of Lewes and its Environs," published December 19th, 1826, which informs us that:

"Two excellent schools, conducted on the Lancastrian plan and supported by voluntary contributions, are established in this town; much both in regard to the origin and success of these institutions is due to the benevolence of John and Robert Chatfield Esqrs., by the former of whom the boys schoolroom was built in 1815 and the girls by the latter in 1816. The gratuitous use of these rooms has been kindly continued up to the present time. We regret, however, to state that the funds of this institution are by no means in a flourishing condition, owing, partly, to the pressure of the times, and somewhat to unworthy feelings and suspicions. The late excellent rector of Westmeston, the Rev. William Campion, whose lamented death took place whilst making a continental tour, was a firm and active supporter of the school and contributed liberally towards its funds, as well from his own purse and from an annuity at his disposal, left by the Rev. Anthony Springett, formerly rector of the parish. The subscription was lost by the death of Mr. Campion and the annuity has since been withdrawn."

As these free schools were worked in connection with the chapel, and at the date of their establishment, and for some years subsequently, there were no National Schools, and, moreover, it is recorded that "at one time half the people of Ditchling were educated there," it does not seem surprising that in the years that followed there should have been so great a number of dissenters in the town, considering the size of the place. Let us, however, accord to the brothers John and Robert Chatfield, whom we may regard as the pioneers of education in Ditchling, all due honour for their efforts in this direction. The tombs of the two brothers will be found side by side in the chapel yard.

After the termination of Mr. Bennett's ministry—

"Two young men from Lewes then supplied the pulpit for two years, one of whom afterwards rose to distinction."

These two were Henry Acton and William Browne, fellow apprentices in Baxter's printing office at Lewes. Henry Acton, during his ministry, seems to have studied under Dr. Morrell at Brighton; in 1823 he went to Walthamstowe, and after that to Exeter, where he remained for twenty-three years.

He was succeeded at Ditchling by a Mr. Kite, after whom came John Owen Squier, and in succession Mr. William Stevens, Gideon Duplock, and James Kennaday, and in 1830 a Mr. Esdaile, who published some lectures; his ministry, however, lasted only two years, and he was succeeded by the Rev. George Withall, who afterwards wrote :—

"When I went there (1832) my engagement included the charge of a school on the Lancastrian system; this and the chapel duties together I found an arduous and anxious undertaking. . . . Pleasant associations are connected in my memory with Ditchling, its people and surroundings, notably the famed South Downs, over which I frequently experienced the effects of a ramble. . . . The families connected with the chapel at that time consisted mainly of Mr. and Mrs. James Brown, Aunt Molly, and Mary the niece, Mrs. Chatfield, the Martens, Turners, Mercers, Woods, Burtenshaws, Rowlands, Kensetts, etc. Mr. James Brown was the leader in congregational affairs and after his decease Mr. Edward Turner was the most active man. Dear old Aunt Molly . . . to know her and enjoy her sympathy was like finding a refreshing stream in a thirsty land."

The Mr. James Browne above-mentioned belonged to a family long connected with Ditchling; we have already mentioned them in connection with our notes on "Place House," their home.

A peculiar feature of Ditchling is the burial place of this family, a small piece of ground scarcely larger than the space covered by a small room; adjacent to, but divided from, the chapel yard, by the path connecting Lewes Road and East End Lane, locally known as "The Twitten." Mr. James Browne was for forty years treasurer of the Ditchling Library Society (broken up about ten years since, and which contained some three or four hundred volumes). He died January 10th, 1834, aged 64, and his memorial stone will be found in the miniature graveyard with others of his family. Of this interesting spot Horsfield informs us that—

"It is decorated with flowers and shrubs of the most pleasing kind, flowers of varied hue and character, emblematic of the individuals over whose relics they blossom, and shrubs whose evergreen leaves seem to tell of their immortality."

And to this day the burial place is well tended, and the precincts of the historic chapel and the dwelling-house adjoining originally intended for a resident minister, but now occupied by the caretaker, present always a neat appearance. It is interesting to notice that Gideon Algernon Mantell, the geologist, who was also an accomplished litterateur, wrote some stanzas on this spot.

Of "Aunt Molly," as she was called, it is recorded that "at eighty-seven she could write a beautifully clear hand." She is described as being "a venerable looking old lady, with her close cap and her muslin kerchief pinned down in front."

In her younger days she kept a school in the old house which we have so often mentioned; the room where she taught the three R's was that on the first floor, with the large window overlooking the road, and we have heard one of her former pupils (herself now over eighty) relate how, when there was a funeral or a wedding, "Aunt Molly" would allow them to watch the people go in or come out of the church.

The inscription to Aunt Molly is as follows:—

"Erected to the memory of Mrs. Mary Browne who died the 17th Febry. 1845 in the 89th year of her age. Mary Browne was the daughter of John and Ann Browne grandaughter of Peter Browne who was buried in this part of his garden, who gave this ground to be used by the family as a place of burial."

And adjoining it is the headstone of "Peter Browne draper, grocer, etc. of this parish who died May 5th 1774 aged 86.".

Continuing the history of the chapel, we are told that for three years after 1834 the chapel had no settled minister; but in 1837 Thomas Grimes, formerly a Quaker, came, but remained only three years, and again embraced his early faith. He was succeeded by Mr. Tinwood (1840), and in 1841 Mr. Gilbert, of Northiam, who after eleven years, "wanting a wider sphere in which to work for truth and righteousness," emigrated to New Zealand. In 1852 the Rev. Alexander Macdougal became minister, and in 1855 Mr. Moir "for one year." The next minute referring to this matter, we are told, is 1864, when "The thanks of the Church are given to Messrs. Albert Burtenshaw, Robert and Alfred Turner, for conducting services this year, when they had no minister." For nearly thirty years after this the records are very scanty; the preachers and number of those who took part in the anniversary services and some of the repairs are all that can be gathered.

The building was renovated and reseated in 1887. The present trustee is Mr. J. W. Brooker, but there is now no resident minister. A noteworthy event in Ditchling, however, is the anniversary, which takes place on the first Sunday in July, and usually in ideal summer weather; then as of yore come visitors from all parts of the county to join in the services.

CHAPTER X.

THE "JERNEL" OF A DITCHLING MAN.

A SOMEWHAT remarkable man was John Burgess, who lived at, and carried on business in Ditchling at the latter end of the eighteenth and beginning of the nineteenth century. We have said "carried on business," but businesses would seem to be a more correct definition, if we may judge from the records which he has left us of his doings.

These consist of a diary extending over a period embracing the years from 1785 to 1815, still in the possession of the family, and it is by the permission of the late Mr. Frank W. Burgess, of Ringmer, who was a great-grandson of the above-named John Burgess, that we are enabled to quote from it.

An interesting paper on this diary appears in Suss. Arch. Coll., Vol. xl., edited by Mr. John Sawyer.

The "Jernel," as the diary is termed by its writer, gives many interesting details of life in Ditchling in his day, recalls many names, no longer familiar, except by tradition, and mentions with frequency such places as Court Gardens and The Jointure, which he spells "Curt Gardens" and "The Jintler." He also mentions The Rookery, where some of the Chatfields lived, a house no longer in existence, but the position of which may still be located, as the garden in which it stood and the gateway leading into the same still remain, but all trace of the house is gone, though it has been pulled down but a very few years.

Judging from the various trades in which John Burgess engaged, we cannot be very far wrong in saying that there were few things which he could not turn his hand to, and that with advantage, such as currying, wool-dealing, harness and rope making, appraising, brewing, grave-digging, haymaking, harvesting, bookbinding, carpentering; these and many other business pursuits did he engage in by turns.

Scarcely less active was he in religious duties. We have already noted his selection as Elder in 1783 by the Baptists of Ditchling, and he tells us that he frequently preached in the Meeting House there, and elsewhere in the county.

Here are some of the business transactions recorded as taking place. Friday, February 25th, 1785:—

"I went to Mr. Tailer at St. John's Common with a pair of breeches for W. Tailer, from thence to Mr. Buckman's Little Wat Hall (Little Ote Hall) with a pair. Eat some breakfast there, then to Mr. Knight at ye tanyard, then to Mr. Drawbridges Scains Hill, stopd dinner there, then to Lindfield to meet Mr. Garten with a pr and went to Wm. Woods to put them on, spent 9d."

On another occasion he says:—

"Went to ye Purchert to car Mr. Billinghurst a pr new breeches, received £1 1s. 0d. on account, bot two pr new breeches of him at 7s. 6d., and are to make him another pr new ones on that ac. In the afternoon went to Huntlers after sheep skins, etc. Had Henry Woods horse 7d."

Mr. Burgess had a good connection in the tailoring line. Another entry informs us—

"This morning went to the Jintler with a pr breeches for Mr. Wood doe at £1 7s. 0d. they fit him well the best that he had any before."

On another occasion he "paid the Barber for two quarters shaving all that was due 4s. etc." and again "settled accounts with Mr. Street paid him for 2 quarters shaving due last Midsummer Day, he paid me for altering a pair of breeches 4 pence," etc.

"Went to ye Bull to a baffling mach for sute of cloths and gloves of mine" and again "Went to ye Bull raffled away some gloves." "Bot a coate to ware every day

3s. 6d. Bot a pr of spackled stockings for myself. Richard Edwards (his brother in law) gave me a pr plated shoe buckles."

(Those were the days of knee breeches and low shoes.)

Amongst miscellaneous purchases on several different occasions he tells us that he " Bot a coat and vest of Richard Burgess 3s. 6d." " Bot an old coat gave 2s. 6¾d. for it," and at " a sale of Mary Hamman's furniture down at Mr. Wardens house, bot a settle for my corner @ 4d. and several other tryfils."

On one occasion when in Lewes he " went to Harbens (an ironmonger's) bot a cast iron boat to Greace Rushes in 8s.," also he informs us on another occasion that he " got a bundle of Candle Rushes in a pon a few fields off Huntlers."

The following entry, dated Friday, May 2nd, 1786, is interesting:—

"This morning John Goddens sweeped or chimily and I begin to burn coal to-day. Bot a pr grates of Harebrook Gave him 6s. for them, was almost new," etc.

A certain entry records that Mr. Burgess—

" Went to Lewes to ye Setting at the White Hart to take out a Licence to dress leather gave twenty shillings for it."

And later on:—

" Went to Lewes to pay sum duty for leather, rid great part of ye way home in Jintler teame."

And again:—

" Went to Lewes to get a Liceance to sell gloves."

" Work for Mr. Godard the Brassure mending his forge bellows."

" Went to Lewes with some wool to Mr. Chatfield, fine wool at £0 5s. 0d. per pack.

These and many other transactions did he engage in. Social events and pleasure excursions also are frequently noted, and here is one which seems a little startling when we remember that it was made by the Elder of a Baptist community:—

Tues. Aug: 1st, 1786. "Went to Brighthelmstone Races."

And we feel tempted to enquire why he went with the crowd, was he on business or pleasure bent, or did he go as a racecourse missioner? It is probable, however, that the crowd which assembled at the races in those days bore no comparison with that which congregates at the meetings now, and could John Burgess see the riff-raff which fills Brighton during the "Sussex Fortnight," the sight would cause him to hold up his hands in pious horror. On one occasion when he "went up to Brighthelmstone," he "washed in ye sea."

He was a frequent visitor to the Rookery; thus he says:—

"Went to Mr. Chatfields at the Rookery about 2 o'clock, had a good piece of boyled beef one rost duck and plum pudden for dinner, we had a pot of good punch and smoaked a pipe or to."

The diarist invariably gives a list of the eatables, and very frequent are the references to punch; he describes a harvest supper at the Rookery, "a great company being present" that he "supt in ye hall" and "we had two large bowles of punch and upwards and came away between 12 and 1 o'clock."

And also when transacting business with a Mr. Young, at "Arndle," the two after dinner drank "Half crownd Bowl of punch and two pots of strong beer."

On Friday, March 14th, 1788, "Went to Fryersoake to a Bull Bait, plenty of Wine and punch all the afternoon," and that there were a great many people.

On Wed: Aug: 19th, 1788, "Went to Brighthelmstone to see many Divertions on account of the Rial Family that is the Duke of Yorks Berthday Cricketing, Stool Ball, Foot Ball, Dancing, Fireworks, etc. two large beasts rosted upon the hill, a large quantity of bread and strong beer given with the beef." The information is also given that it was "a fine day," and "some saide there was 20,000 people."

On one occasion when in Lewes, Mr. Burgess records having seen a freak in the animal world thus:—

"Went to ye Crown Lewes to see a very remarkable ox that was their for show, it was like other oxen in every respect except its head and that had only one horne, growed strait out of its poul of about 3 ft 8 inches or near 4 feet and was so long as to prevent his grasing so that he cant get his mouth to ye ground so that he is oblidge to be fed with bran etc. in a difrant manner, he is about five years old bread in Scotland gave 2d. to see him."

There are several references to cricket matches, but the details given are meagre; thus when recording a journey to Lindfield and Chailey, he remarks:—

"There was a cricket Match at Lindfield Common between Lingfield in Surrey and all the County of Sussex. Soposed to be upwards of 2,000 people."

It would have been interesting to know which side won, but this information is not vouchsafed to us.

A journey to London is recorded when he says:—

"Got up about 3 o'clock and set off with Mr. and Mrs. Drawbridge we stopd at Godstone and bated at Mrs. Day's, got to London about 4, eat my supper at the Spur and then went to Talbot in to sleep."

The business which took him to the Metropolis seems to have been "an assembly."

Under date Thursday, January 19th, 1786, Mr. Burgess notes his doings as follows:—

"This forenoon went to Keymer with several people in pursuit of the person soposed to have robbed Mrs. Browns shop, it was soposed he was concealed in old Mooryes House and by virtue of a warrant we serched his house but did not find the man, but found several things soposed to have been stollen, a quantity of wheat in the chafe and a large quantity of old timber concealed in a very Secret Place upon the ceiling over the chamber," etc. "A great number of people was there," etc.

Mr. Burgess makes no further reference to the above incident, but from other sources we have gathered the following sequel:—

The person alluded to was a man named Fox, a worker at the lime kilns, and if report speaks truly, a man of enormous strength; on one occasion, it is said, he held back the wheel of a loaded waggon which was proceeding down Ditchling Borstal, the skid pan having broken. He was arrested for the above-named robbery, and many of the articles were found in a barn near Hurst, since known as Foxe's hole, we suppose from this circumstance. The man was tried, found guilty, and as the punishment for stealing any article over the value of 1s. was, in those days, death, he suffered the extreme penalty at Horsham, where the Assizes were then held.

Another noteworthy entry in the "Jernel" is that recorded January 30th, 1789:—

"I paide Mr. Attree five shillings what I subscribed toward the Sunday Scool at Ditchling, this is the first year of its being established" (at Ditchling).

Some extracts relating more or less to funerals are not a little gruesome. Thus in January, 1786, he says:

"Master Hallett and I did open a Steen Grave wherein Mrs. Chatfield was buried in ye year 1766 she was 54 years of age, we took the coffin out and set it in the Meeting House all night, we opened it, nothing to be seen but a perfect skeleton, she was Grandmother to Miss Sally Mott who is to be buried to-morrow."

On the following day he "was diging a grave for Mr. Daniel Pannett," and he also informs us that—

"Sally Mott was brought from the Rookery to be buried, that the service was performed by candle-light. There was a great many people. Snow in ye morning, freeze in ye evening."

In July of the same year he "was assisting in opening a Steen grave in order to enlarge it for to put Mr. Chatfield in, it was his father's grave and he had been buried fifty years, the coffin was very much decayed but not so much but we could see the Date etc."

On the following day he records that the funeral of Mr. Chatfield took place, and that "the meeting was very full of people."

Mrs. Chatfield, buried in 1766, was Sarah, daughter of Joseph Looker, of Ditchling, and widow of Robert, elder son of Robert, the founder of the chapel, while the Mr. Chatfield buried in 1786 was Michael, of Court Gardens.

In the same year (1786), John Burgess records the funeral of Mr. Peter Marten, at which there was a very large number of spectators, and that Mr. Drowley preached the sermon.

On 29th March, 1787, he was "diging grave for Mrs. Boadle," whom he describes as 82 years of age, and "a Woman of an acceeding good character."

In August, 1787, he records the death of Mr. Agate, and that Mr. Billinghurst's vault was opened to bury him in; also that Mr. Evershed preached the sermon.

On November 9th, 1787, he writes:—

"Work in ye Meeting House, Mr. Rowland made an end of seting up of Toombs. He and 2 of his men came last Thursday. Set up 1 for Looker Chatfield 1 for Mrs. Boadle 1 for Mr. Joseph Chatfield and Mrs. His wife etc."

Looker Chatfield, son of Michael, of Court Gardens, by Lucy (daughter of Joseph) Looker his wife, died 30th March, 1773, aged 21. Mr. Joseph Chatfield (son of Robert and Sarah, formerly Looker his wife) died 17th June, 1784, aged 47, and Elizabeth his wife died 12th February, 1776, aged 38.

A note in the diary records "diging a grave to bury Mrs. Wood in."

THE HISTORY OF DITCHLING.

A monumental inscription in the burial ground is in memory of Lucy, daughter of Michael Chatfield, of Court Gardens, and wife of Mr. Thomas Wood, of London, died 10th January, 1788, aged 34.

In connection with the name "Looker," it is interesting to note that in 1670 James Looker, of Ditchling, blacksmith, made a clock for Cliffe Church, costing £5 10s. 0d., the great wheel of which is now in the Museum at Lewes Castle, while a note in Vol. xxxvii., p. 199, Suss. Arch. Coll., states that one of the original wheels and frame of the clock were in 1889 still in existence in the church tower.

On Sunday, July 13th, 1788, Mr. Burgess says:—

"In the evening my father in law was buried at Ditchling in the same grave that his last wife my mother in law was buried in, he was 75 years of age Mr. Evershed preached. He died at Wisboro Green, was brought from there to-day in a waggon brought to the Bull, was card. into the Bull parler, proceed to meeting about 7 o'clock, after service we went with Mr. Evershed to the Bull smoked with him there," etc.

(John Burgess's father-in-law's name was Edwards.)

We have before noted that John Burgess was a preacher, and he records frequent visits to Crawley, Waldron, Heathfield, etc., on Sundays, his object being to hold forth to the dissenting congregations of those places.

On a special occasion, viz., Wednesday, November 5th, 1788, he says:—

"In the afternoon went to the Purchert, there was a Meeting kept there on account of Gunpowder Plot, I preached a sermon upon psalms 107. 31, there was one hymn sung after sermon."

But though a dissenter, John Burgess was no bigot, and would occasionally attend church. Thus, on Christmas Day, 1788, he remarks:—

"Went to Church to hear our Mr. Jackson and in

the afternoon went to Keymer Church to hear Mr. Turner, he preach a good sermon in my opinion."

And again on Thursday, April 23rd, 1789:—

"In the forenoon went to church to hear Mr. Jackson and in ye afternoon went to Street to hear Mr. Morgan, it was a day set apart as a day of Thanksgiving for the King's recovery from a state of indisposition in the evening our Town was illuminated on the occation."

Mr. Jackson was either Vicar or Curate of Wivelsfield, we are not certain which, but he frequently preached in Ditchling Church also in those days.

On another occasion, a Sunday, John Burgess records after having been to "ye Purchert Meeting," and preached a sermon himself—

"Went from thence to Chapple Church (Chiltington) heard Mr. Rideout Preach, after service there was a Vestry to settle about Sarah Parsons living with me to learn to Glover, we agreed for her to stay one year and a quarter and to alow her 6d. per week to pay her quarters with, the parish to alow her 2s. 6d. to live upon."

And here we will conclude our notes on the "Jernel" of John Burgess. He emigrated to America, and some letters in the possession of his family give his impressions of the country of his adoption, and in which he died.

THE CROSS, PLUMPTON.

CHAPTER XI.

THE NEIGHBOURHOOD.

THE surroundings of Ditchling are worthy of much closer attention than we are able to give in one short chapter on the subject. Many charming walks and interesting places abound in the immediate neighbourhood, and should be sought out by all who have the time and inclination.

And we turn first to that range of hills, the South Downs, whose bold but varied outlines and deep coombes form so picturesque a background to the views from the weald, and from the summits of which so many magnificent and extensive views may be obtained.

As regards East Sussex, the Downs reach their highest point in Ditchling Beacon, which has an elevation of 813 feet above the level of the sea, being, however, exceeded in height by two other points in West Sussex, viz., Linch Down, which has an elevation of 818 feet, and Duncton Down, 837 feet.

The Beacon is approached from the weald by a zigzag road, familiarly called the Bostal or Borstal (a way up a hill), which winds round the heights (here somewhat precipitous) and attains the summit a short distance eastward of the Beacon and encampment.

This fine hill has always been and will be a most interesting spot, not only on account of the lovely view which may be enjoyed by those who climb to its summit, but from its associations.

Before the days of the electric telegraph, the hill was an important signalling station, and on its summit stood an immense scaffold, in height about fifty feet, visible for many miles distant. It was the duty of a number of the Royal Engineers to transmit messages from this scaffold by signal to distant places, but with the advent of the telegraph there was no longer any use for the Beacon as a signalling station, and the scaffold was removed.

There can be little doubt that a Beacon fire blazed here to alarm and raise the district when England was threatened with an invasion from the great Spanish Armada in 1588.

And here in recent years have two memorable fires been lighted by ready and willing hands and blazed forth, not as signals of alarm, but of public rejoicing, viz., in 1887 and 1897, to celebrate the two Jubilees of Queen Victoria.

A familiar and everyday feature of this and the neighbouring hills is the Southdown shepherd.

A tall, gaunt man, usually; there he stands, leaning on his Pyecombe crook, and by his side his faithful dog, while near at hand are the flock browsing on the short sweet herbage, which is believed by many to be in a great measure responsible for the excellent quality and flavour of the mutton into which the animals are converted, and which is justly famed all the world over. Mr. John Brown, senr., late of Ditchling Court Farm, was, we believe, one of the largest flockmasters on the South Downs.

Another sight, but one which is becoming more rare every year, is a team of oxen ploughing, and why this animal is falling into disuse for this purpose it would be hard to tell, but probably before long it will no longer be seen on the Downs.

The wheatear, or English ortolan, a bird much esteemed, abounds on these hills in the autumn, and is said to frequent the district for a certain fly which feeds on the wild thyme. The shepherds are principally concerned in trapping them, and as many as two thousand dozen are stated to have been annually caught in years gone by, a ready sale being always found for them. Of this little bird Charles II. is said to have been very fond, and at a dinner given by the Earl of Dorset to the King and his brother the Duke of York, no less a number than twenty dozen of them were consumed.

Of the view from the summit of Ditchling Beacon we can say but little, it must be seen to be appreciated, but we may say that it is one the peaceful beauty of which is not easily surpassed, embracing as it does, on the one hand, the greater part of rural Sussex, and on the other, a magnificent prospect of the waters of the Channel, and in very clear weather even the shores of the Isle of Wight.

Near at hand is the well-wooded park of the Earl of Chichester (Stanmer), by the wall of which for a considerable distance runs the old coach road, now in many places only a rugged track across the Downs.

Further to the eastward is an extensive table land, known as Plumpton Plain, a very unusual feature of the South Downs, and where some of the incidents of the Battle of Lewes are traditionally believed to have transpired. On the escarpment of the hill near at hand, and, to be exact, at a spot directly opposite Plumpton Place, is an immense cross incised in the turf. The device seems to have been originally a " cross moline," and when bare to the chalk must have been visible for many miles. It is believed to be a relic of the Battle of Lewes, and some have ventured the theory that it marks the spot where the Baron's army, under Simon de Montfort, ascended the hills prior to the battle. Another and more likely theory is to the effect that it was formed by the monks of Southover as a memorial of those slain in the battle, that distant travellers, seeing the great white cross on the hillside, might offer their prayers for the repose of those who had perished in that deadly strife.

A close examination of this device will prove that originally the arms of the cross were each, from the centre, about fifty feet long, but the lower one has been shortened somewhat by reason of the mass of loose earth which has washed down and so partly filled up the trench. Being now overgrown with turf, it is visible only under certain circumstances of light, and from various points, notably Street Hill on a summer evening, when the air is very clear and the shadows begin to deepen in the coombes; while a nearer view may be obtained from the lane which turns southward from Plumpton Racecourse into the Lewes Road.

And here may be noted Plumpton Church, standing solitary in the fields, and a weird and remarkably loud echo may at times be heard at a spot on the road immediately opposite the building, and should be tested.

To the east is the ancient Manor House of Plumpton, which is surrounded by a moat, and a glimpse of this, one of the loveliest pieces of scenery in the neighbourhood, should certainly not be missed. Anciently the home of the Mascalls, it was Leonard Mascall who, in the reign of Henry VIII., is said to have introduced the first carp into England, placing them in the moat here, where it is said the fish abound to-day.

And here formerly was the tapestry now in the Barbican at Lewes Castle.

Though divided up into tenements, and now the abode of peasantry, Plumpton Place, almost hidden away in this sequestered spot, preserves its old time appearance, the moat running all round the house save where the drawbridge should be, and which is replaced by a causeway.

On the north side, the moat broadens out into a large mill pond, over the peaceful waters of which glide some snow-white swans.

The stream which rises here drives several water mills on its journey towards the Ouse, of which river it is a considerable tributary.

A short distance to the north-east is Chiltington, a small hamlet and chapelry of Westmeston, and should

THE HISTORY OF DITCHLING.   137

be visited, not only on account of its picturesque beauty, of which it possesses a considerable share, but from the fact that it contains two " decayed mansions," Stantons and Chapel House, which were for generations the residences of the Chatfields and Challoners.

The tiny chapel has slight traces of Norman architecture, and stands in a small graveyard, in which there are no graves, but a noble yew tree said to be older than the chapel itself, and beneath the spreading branches of which is a comfortable seat.

At Westmeston are two very large yew trees, one fast going to decay. The quaint Early English woodwork of the church porch should be noted.

The interior walls of the church, having been rebuilt, retain not a trace of the beautiful frescoes discovered in 1862. For a description of these we must refer the reader to Suss. Arch. Coll., Vol. xvi., pp. 1-19, where the matter is dealt with very fully and illustrated by engravings.

In a coombe adjacent to the village is a plantation in the form of an enormous letter V, which is a striking land-mark for many miles distant, and was planted as a memorial of Queen Victoria's 1887 Jubilee by H. C. Lane, Esq., on whose estate, Middleton, it is situated.

At Streat is an Elizabethan mansion, Streat Place, once the home of the ancient family of Dobell, ancestors of the present occupier, General Fitzhugh. There is a legend attached to this house which runs thus:—A cavalier being hard pressed by Cromwell's Ironsides, rode one day across the Downs and valleys into the house, and disappeared up the chimney in the ancient hall for ever.

The panelling in the drawing-room is a beautiful specimen of Jacobean work, and there are several fireplaces dating from the same period.

Some memorials will be found in the church here, principally to the families of Dobell and Gott, and also some interesting iron grave slabs in the floor of the nave. In the buttresses of the churchyard wall are some polished flints, the varied and beautiful colours of which are worthy of examination.

Wivelsfield should also be visited. Ote Hall in that parish is a notable house, and was formerly the home of the Godmans, and here Queen Elizabeth once sojourned when making a Royal progress through the county.

The church stands in a picturesque and well-kept churchyard, which commands a good southward view.

The building should be examined, as it contains some interesting memorials, notably to the names of Richbell, More, Middleton, etc.

Keymer Church, which has been practically rebuilt in recent years, retains its apsidal chancel, one of very few in Sussex.

At the east end of the south aisle of this church is a memorial window to "the ancient family of Turner, who had held Oldland in Keymer parish for 300 years," but as Oldland was sold in 1863, the period given is not quite correct, though nearly so.

Clayton, a tiny village under the Downs, has a church whose chancel arch is evidently Saxon. Some beautiful frescoes were uncovered on the walls of the nave in 1893, and represent the doom and other subjects, and a very full description of these will be found in Suss. Arch. Coll., Vol xl.

Pyecombe Church, in the same neighbourhood, also contains some features of interest, including a leaden font.

Hurstpierpoint, about three miles westward of Ditchling, has a fine modern church built on the site of the ancient and smaller church of St. Lawrence, which had fallen into decay, the present spacious edifice being erected about the middle of the last century.

A ramble through Danny Park should also be enjoyed, and may be extended through Newtimber and on to Poynings, which nestles under the Dyke Hills,

THE HISTORY OF DITCHLING. 139

and in which parish is the remarkable chasm known as the "Devil's Dyke," the legend attaching to this spot being well known. The fine old cruciform church, with its massive square tower, should not be passed by. It has several fine Perpendicular windows, but the monuments to the noble Lords of Poynings and the Montague family have suffered much from spoliation.

And to go further afield we may mention Lindfield and Cuckfield, the "Place" of the latter being the "Rookwood" of Ainsworth's romance.

The view from Cuckfield churchyard southward is a very fine one, and should certainly be seen by all who visit the neighbourhood, as it cannot be surpassed anywhere in the county.

DITCHLING SUBSIDY ROLLS.

The names of the earliest inhabitants are contained in these Rolls for the Rape of Lewes under the head of the Hundred of Street.

In the Roll for 1296 under "Villata de Lyndefeld et Burle," the only local name that occurs is Joh. Atte Ree, and in the Roll for the "Villata de Lofeld," 1327 ($\frac{189}{3}$) " Rectore de Dichenyng" appears as having paid 2s. on the collection of a twentieth. The Poll Tax of 2 Rich. II. ($\frac{189}{41}$), 1378, gives under the head of "Villata de Dychenynge" only the unmarried people. The "Comunarii disponsati" were "Commoners betrothed" as distinguished from "Comunarii maritati" or "Commoners married," who were treated differently and only paid the same amount (4d.) including their wives. "Soli non disponsati" were single men, not even betrothed; and in some places "Soli et sole" single men and single women occur, and in others "Soli" cover women as well as men. When "vidua" does not occur the women were spinsters and not widows.

The Act fixing the rates for the Poll Tax is enrolled on Parliament Roll 2 Rich. II. pt. 2, and lays down very clearly the amount to be levied from each class of persons. The other Roll of 2 Rich. II. ($\frac{189}{36}$) is a mere fragment, and does not contain Ditchling.

The Roll for 13 Hen. IV. ($\frac{189}{63}$), 1412, on £20 per an. and over, only mentions: "Thomas Earl of Arundel paying £12 10s. 0d. for his Manor of Dichenyng and Middleton," and Thomas Camoys £6 for "his Manor of Dedelyng."

The Rolls for 15 Hen. VIII. ($\frac{189}{119}$), 1524, 3 Edw. VI. ($\frac{190}{235}$), 1549, and 18 Eliz. ($\frac{190}{299}$), 1575, do not give the names of parishes, but only the Hundreds. The Rolls of 37 Hen.

VIII. ($\frac{190}{218}$), 1546, 5 Eliz. ($\frac{190}{274}$), 1562, 43 Eliz. ($\frac{190}{342}$), 1600, and 21 James I. ($\frac{191}{372}$), 1623, give the parishes.

"Villata de Dychenynge" in Hund de Strete.

2 Rich. II., 1378-9.

Rado Petybon	Tannatores (tanners)
Rico Blakemor	
Johne Coupe	
Waltero Cromp	Cissores pannorum (cloth tailors)
Robto Taillor	
Johne Atte Wyke	Pistor panis (bread baker)
Robto Berd	Tector domorum cum stramine (thatcher of houses with straw)
Waltero Wilde	de albator (white tawzer or dresser of white leather)
Comunar dispons... ...	Joh Mey
(commoners betrothed)	Robto Mathen
	Rads Atte Wike
	Willo atte Crofte
	Thom. Leg.
	Rico Balcombe
	Walt atte Wyke
	Joh atte Ree
	Joh Cook
	Walt Chyntynge
	Simon Grubbe
	Robt Bakere
	Joh Bette
	Tho. Drew
	Walt Twycemot
	Walt Sligh
	Rob. Wadebrok
	John Wodelond
	Rad Wadnage
	John Brown
	Will Wadnage

Soli non dispons (single men and women not betrothed)

Walt Drounyng
Tho. Hurdone
Ric Raynole
Joh Steer
Rad Rolfe
John Atte Bowre
Walt Cur
Joh Alvard
John Smyth
Tho. Reghemen
Rich. Grigge
Simon Osemund
Walt Bedil
Ric. Symonel
Walt Grigge
Wil. Ffullere
John Dorkinge
Rad Sket
John Coup
Walt Wadelond
Joh Wadelond
Joh Raynold
Rad Rolf
Simon Skep
Joh Birchop
Agn Chyntyng
Wil. Skyronde
Edith Blakestre
Alice Webbe
Alice Wodelond
Alice Southbrok
Rad Cadele
Joh Brounyng
Joh Dymmoke
John Grigge
Alice Bedil
Joh Rolf
Isabell Sprot
Emma Coup
Alice Rolerh ?

HUNDRED OF STRETE (extracts only).
14 & 15 HEN. VIII., 1523-4.

Rob Chele
Tho. Hyder
Symon Hyder
Will. A'More
Joh A'More
John Marten
John Chele
Tho Peckden
Joh Fuller
Tho Owton
Rich Alcoke
Rich Chatfield
Tho Chatfield
Tho Chatfield Junr.
Tho Chelley
Tho Hentye
Joh Leperd
Rich Markewyke
Will Chatfeld
Rich Pykenoll
Tho. Holmwode
Roger Thurston
Tho. Pykecombe
Tho. A'More Sen.
John Chatfield Sen.
John Chatfield Junr.
Roger Faulkner
Gerard Holcomb
Henry Hyder
Joh Pardon
Joh At Ree
Rich Dumbrell
Alex Pan
Rich At Ree
Tho At Ree
John At Tree
Tho Dumbrell
Will Dumbrell
Tho At Ree Jun
Rich Hether
Roger Chele
Rich Mascall
Joh Debarnarde (a Frenchman)
Mat Agas
John A'Wode
Rich Esterfield
Tho. Looke
Will Freman
Joh A'More
Rich Ferell
Joh Alchorn
John Godman
Peter Denett
Nich. Challinor
Ro. Hollingdale
Phil. Jenner
Joh Vynall
Tho. Jenner

DYCHELYNGS
37 HEN. VIII., 1546.

Joh Michelbourne
Edw. Gynner
Jemis Godley
Rich Cowper
Hen Hyder
Steph. A'Wod
Margery Whyttyng
Tho. A'More
Rich Marten
John Townyng

Rog Piknoll
John Ferall
Rich Ferall
John Smith
Rog. Benkin
Will A'More
Nich. Lysney

Margery Stere
Tho. Alchorn
Edw. Wykham
Rich. Allen
Tho Parson
John Turner
Steph. Pollyngton

STRETE HUNDRED (the whole of it).
3 EDW. VI., 1549.

Gerard Onsty
Joh Brete
John Ilman
Rich Gaston
Tho. Brete
Edw. Balcomb
Will Lynfeld
John Payn
Joh Besall
Tho Nunam
Tho Gason
Cornel Ard (alien)
Tho. Luxford
Rich Michelborn
Joh Pardan
Joh Cheley
Joh Michelborn
Steph Pollyngton
Steph A'Wod
Joh Ferall
Rich Coper
James Godley
Joh Smyth
Tho Parson
Cornells Burton (alien)
Rosse Shomaker
Henry Hider
Tho Allchorn
Will Colman
Joh Hull

Rob. Hesman
Joh Brian
Hen Payn
Walter Feldewyke
Richard Juseley
Jer. Chamberlyn
John Bridge
Rich. Bridge
Rich. Bakesell
Rich Nunam
Nich. Jenkyn
Herman Tulli (alien)
Joh Culpeper Esq.
Rich Savage
Rich. Button
Tho. Owton
Joh Mascall
Rob Proour
Symon Potter
Roger Marten
Rich. Hollingdale
John Fawkenor
Joh Gere
Nich. Challoner
Rich Ford
Rich Warren
Tho. Godman
Rich Motrion (alien)
Walter A'More

DYCHENINGE

5 Eliz., 1562

Rich Hyder
Nich Alchorn
Rich Michelbourne
Rob. Picknoll
Tho. Pollington
Jas. Godley
Jo. Smythes
Tho. Childe
Rich Coper
Jo. Malisbie
Tho. Alchorn

Tho. A'More
Edw. Michelbourne
Rich Walshe
Walter Hyder
Geo. Undrell
Ph. Feyrall
Steph. Pollington
Juliane Cogger wid.
Nich. Ubbard
Jerard Johnson

STRETE HUND. (extract).

(In Lands).

18 Eliz., 1575.

John á Wood
Richard Michelbourne Jun
Henry Poole Esq.
Stephen Pollington
John At. Ree
Walter á More
Thomas Godman

Thomas Lucas
Margaret Chatfield wid
Robert Chatfield
Nicholas Chatfield
John Pardon
Nicholas Ferall
Alice King wid

DITCHLING.

43 Eliz., 1600.

Henry Hyder Gent in goods   Stephen Pollington in lands
Sackvill Porter Gent in lands   William Gun in lands

DITCHLING

21 James, 1623.

Robert Chatfield in lands   Mr Sackville Porter in lands
Mr Henry Hyder in lands

DITCHLING WILLS AT LEWES
1541 TO 1640

1549	William More
1542	George Stere
1545	Walter Stere
1549	William Trendle
1545	Nicholas Whiting
1549-51	Stephen A'Wood
1550	Thomas Joner (Admon)
1550	William Trendyle
1554	John Fayrall
1554	Nicholas Hyder (Admon)
1554	Henry Hyder
1554	Nicholas Lysney
1553	Stephen Pollington
1553	John Rose Clerk (Admon)
1552	Margery Stere wid.
1556	John Trayton
1558	Robert A'Tree Sen. (Admon)
1559-60	Katherine Chandler
1558	Thurstan Hyder (Admon)
1558	William Hubbard
1557-8	Thomas Parsons
1561	Richard Bawcome
1565-6	Philip Beard
1562-3	John Caplen
1568	Richard Coper
1562	Richard Gatlande
1566	Thomas Harrys Clerk (Admon)
1565-8	William Pelling
1561-2	George Renfeld
1561	John Smythe
1566-7	Richard Welche
1573	Henry Cottmell
1572	John Townynge
1578-9	Joan A'Wood
1576	Edward Berd

1578	Roger Benke
1574-5	James Godlyf
1580	Margaret Smithe
1581-2	Thomas Wilson
1588	John Attree
1591	Nicholas A'Wood
1590-1	Stephen Attree
1588	John Dennett
1590	Eleana Doppe wid
1589	Edward Knight yeo.
1591	Thomas Paine
1587	Richard Virrold Sen.
1593	Mercy Crasbye wid.
1595	John Cooper
1595-6	John Cooper yeo.
1592	Richard Hider yeo.
1592-3	Margaret Mawsbye wid.
1594	John Pardon
1593-4	Gregory Pardon
1596	Robert Smyth
1593	John Underhill Jun.
1592	Richard Woore
1593	John Waterman
1594-6	William Willett
1599	Thomas A'More
1598	Henry Beard
1597	Richard Gatland
1598	Walter Godley
1598	John Gibbe
1598	Constance Hawes wid.
1600-1.	John Hardinge
1598	Richard Nicholas
1600	Henry Gatland weaver
1600	Anne Shelley
1602	John Button
1603	Thomas Chatfield
1606	John Alchin
1607	Thomas Pechten Blacksmith
1608	Henry Payne
1605-7	Richard Steere als Towninge

1610	Nicholas A'Woode yeo.
1610	John Attree
1609-10	Eleanor Ferrall spin.
1610-16	Richard Kinge
1609	William Saunders als Wasten
1612	John Boorne
1612	Richard Wilson
1614	George Hubbard
1614	Robert Langford
1612-14	John Smith
1614	Thomas Waterman
1615	William Beard yeo.
1610-15	Thomas Haslegrove yeo.
1615	John Smyth
1618	John A'Wood
1617	Gerard Savadge
1617	Ann Savadge wid
1617	Margaret Wood
1618-19	Mary De la Chamber wid.
1620	Andrew Gibbs
1617-20	Iden Holland wid.
1620	Thomas Underhill yeo.
1617-21	Thomas Price Clerk
1625-26	Nicholas Bull
1626	Richard Godley
1626	Nicholas Hubard
1625-6	Agnes Rawoode wid
1624-6	Thomas Soundy
1630	Margaret Coulstocke wid.
1631	Thomas Looker. Smith.
1634	Nicholas A'Wood yeo.
1633	Margaret Bawcombe wid.
1634	Michael Moncke
1634	Henry Moncke
1635-6	Judeth Porter
1635-6	Nicholas Weller yeo.
1637	Margaret Marten wid.
1639	George Beadle
1639	Matthew Darcy yeo.
1639	Thomas Marten

1638 Anne Teynton wid.
1640 John Monger   Shepherd.
1583 John A'Tree
1584 George Underhill
1610 John Verroll

DITCHLING ADMINISTRATORS
1578-1640

1578 John Atree
1579 Alice Tye
1583 John French
1584 John Austen
1585 George Undrell
1589 Thomas Starre
1589 Edmund Nealand
1589 Thomas Boothe
1589 Joan Heaseman wid.
1592 Richard Moore
1592 Richard Hider Sen.
1593 Nicholas Hider
1593 Henry Hider
1593 John Waterman
1594 Nicholas Ubbard
1594 Henry Warren als Deane
1595 John Hother
1596 Henry Knight
1600 John or Thomas Markweeke
1600 Richard Hyder
1601 Nicholas Hider
1603 Richard Gatland
1604 Hugh Rawood Clerk
1605 William Chambers
1606 Thomas Worger
1606 Thomas Welche
1607 Allan Savage
1612 Henry Willett
1612 Mary Nicholas
1613 Walter Crabb
1614 John Verroll

1615	John Binson
1615	Joan Reynold wid.
1615	Stephen Cooper
1616	Richard Cooper
1616	Thomas Tester
1617	John Carden
1617	William Savadge
1619	Richard Gatland
1620	Henry Wood
1620	Joan Nicholas
1625	Richard Virroll
1626	Nicholas Hubbard
1626	John Cheale
1626	Thomas Soundy
1626	John Harris
1627	Richard Hardman
1627	Thomas Waller
1627	John Colman
1627	William Nicholas
1628	Nicholas Soundy
1629	John Soundy
1631	Henry Gibbs.
1631	Thomas Beard
1632	George Weller
1632	Richard Smith
1634	Ann Alchorne wid.
1635	John Jeffrey
1635	John Bateman
1636	Thomas Harvy
1636	John Gardner
1638	Henry Hyder Gent.
1639	Richard Cooper
1640	James Savage
1640	Joane Godly
1640	Sarah Soundy als Savage
1640	John Eede
1641	Anne Luxford als Porter
1641	William Butcher
1641	Abraham Savage
1642	Thomas Peirse

DITCHLING CHURCHWARDENS.

1638—1750.

1638	Mr. Edmund Attree	and	Richard Cooper
1639	Michael Munke	,,	Thomas Harris
1640	Michael Munke	,,	Thomas Harris
1641	Sampson Coulstocke	,,	William Moore
1642	Thomas Godman	,,	Robert Chatfield
1643	Thomas Godman	,,	Peter Marchant
1644	Michael Munke	,,	John Pannett
1645	Mr. Tho. Godman	,,	Michael Munke
1646	Henry Field	,,	William Wisdome
1647	Richard Beale	,,	John Buckewell
1648	Mr. Tho. Luxford	,,	Michael Munke
1649	Edward Pollington	,,	Michael Munke
1650	Tho. Nathily gent	,,	John Coleman
1651	William Soundy	,,	Richard Beale
1652	Richard Marchant	,,	Thomas Field
1653	Richard Marchant	,,	Thomas Field
1654	Mr. Tho. Godman	,,	William Wisdome
1655	Henry Field	,,	Richard Beale
1656	William Chatfield	,,	Nicholas White
1657	Mr. John Hony	,,	Mr. Thomas Nathily
1658	Richard Marchant	,,	John Farnecombe
1659	Richard Marchant	,,	Mr. John Hony
1660	Thomas Field	,,	William Langfourd
1661	John Pannett	,,	Mr. Thomas Natly
1662	Mr. Thomas Nathily	,,	John Pannet
1663	Mr. John Hony	,,	Michael Moncke
1664	Mr. John Hony	,,	Michael Moncke
1665	Roger Nicholas	,,	Thomas Whitman
1665	Roger Nicholas	,,	John Limbrice
1667	John Panet junior	,,	John Dunstall
1668	Mr. Edward Mychill	,,	Richard Morris
1669	Mr. Wickersham	,,	John Jeffrey
1670	Mr. Tho. Geere	,,	George Wood

THE HISTORY OF DITCHLING.

1671	Mr. Tho. Geere	and	John Chatfield
1672	Peter Marchant	,,	William Chatfield
1673	Richard Marchant	,,	John Bearone (Browne?)
1674	Peter Marchant	,,	Edward Harroden
1675	Mr. Thomas Geere	,,	Peter Marchant
1676	Tho. Geere	,,	John Chatfield
1677	John Chatfield	,,	Michael Marten
1678	Henry Monck	,,	Edward Geare
1679	Henry Moncke	,,	John Beale
1680	Henry Moncke	,,	John Beale
1681	Mr. William Scrace	,,	Edward Whitman
1682	Peter Marchant senr.	,,	Peter Marchant junr.
1683	Edward Whiteman	,,	Thomas Limbrest
1684	Thomas Limbrest	,,	Edward Whiteman
1685	Nicholas Marchant	,,	Thomas Limbrest
1686	Nicholas Marchant	,,	Thomas Looker
1687	Nicholas Marchant	,,	Thomas Looker
1688	Nicholas Marchant	,,	Thomas Looker
1689	Anthony Tanner	,,	Richard Jeffrey
1690	Richard Morris	,,	John Brown Junr.
1691	John Brown junr.	,,	Richard Morris
1692	John Brown junr.	,,	Richard Morris
1693	Abraham Beale	,,	Thomas Looker
1694	John Knight	,,	William Betchley
1695	John Knight	,,	William Betchley
1696	John Knight	,,	Iohn Dwite
1697	Charles Geere	,,	William Hartfield
1698	George Wood	,,	John Essex
1699	George Wood	,,	John Essex
1700	Richard Butcher	,,	Nicholas Marchant
1701	Richard Butcher	,,	Nicholas Marchant
1702	Nicholas Marchant	,,	Richard Butcher
1703	Richard Butcher	,,	Nicholas Marchant
1704	Richard Butcher	,,	Nicholas Marchant
1705	Edward Gatland	,,	Edward English
1706	Richard Morris Jun.	,,	James Grinyer
1707	Richard Morris	,,	Edmond Ellyot
1708	Jacob Hubbard	,,	Richard Morris
1709	Jacob Hubbard	,,	Richard Morris
1710	Jacob Hubbard	,,	Richard Morris

THE HISTORY OF DITCHLING.   153

1711	Nicholas Marchant	and	Joseph Looker
1712	Richard Morris	,,	Joseph Looker
1713	Thomas Burt	,,	Edward Tanner
1714	Thomas Burt	,,	Edward Tanner
1715	Edward Tanner	,,	Richard Hamshar
1716	Edward Gatland	,,	Thomas Friend
1717	Edward Gatland	,,	Thomas Friend
1718	Richard Morris Junr.	,,	Joseph Looker
1719	John Fuller	,,	Richard Morris junr.
1720	John Fuller	,,	Richard Morris
1721	John Fuller	,,	Richard Morris
1722	Thomas Berry	,,	William Attreé
1723	William Attree	,,	Richard Morris
1724	William Attree	,,	Richard Morris
1725	George Wood	,,	Richard Morris
1726	George Wood	,,	Richard Morris
1727	George Wood	,,	Richard Morris
1728	Edward Harraden	,,	Richard Morris
1729	Edward Harraden	,,	John Fuller
1730	Joseph Looker	,,	James Wood
1731	Nicholas Gatland	,,	James Wood
1732	Nicholas Gatland	,,	John Seaman
1733	Nicholas Gatland	,,	John Seaman
1734	Nicholas Gatland	,,	Joseph Looker
1735	Nicholas Gatland	,,	Joseph Looker
1736	John Hubbard	,,	Joseph Looker
1737	George Wood	,,	Nicholas Gatland
1738	George Wood	,.	Nicholas Gatland
1739	John Attree	,,	Francis Leney
1740	William Attree	,,	Francis Leney
1741	John Attree	,,	Francis Leney
1742	John Attree	,,	Nicholas Gatland
1743	John Attree	,,	Nicholas Gatland
1744	John Attree	,,	Stephen Elliott
1745	John Attree	,,	Stephen Elliott
1746	John Attree	,,	Stephen Elliott
1747	John Attree	,,	Stephen Elliott
1748	John Attree	,,	James Friend
1749	Anthony Tanner	,,	James Friend
1750	Anthony Tanner	,,	James Friend

ORCHIS.

The following is a list of Orchis found during May, June or July in the neighbourhood of Ditchling, on the Downs or in the Weald and its woods :—

MAY.

Orchis Morio (green-winged Meadow O.), W.*
O. Mascula (early purple O.), Wo., W.
Ophrys Muscifera (Fly Op.), D.
Op. Aranifera (Spider Op.), D.
Listera Ovata (common Tway blade), W., Wo.
Lis. Nidus-Avis (common bird's nest), Wo.
Habenaria albida (small white Habenaria), D.

JUNE.

Orchis ustulata (dwarf dark-winged Or.), D.
Or. latifolia (marsh Or.), W.
Or. masculato (spotted palmate Or.), W.
Gymnadenia conopsea (fragrant Gymnadenia), D.
Habenaria viridis (green Habenaria), D.
Hab. bifolia (butterfly Hab.), D.
Aceras anthropophora (green man Or.), W., D.
Ophrys apifera (bee Op.), D.
Epipactis palustris (marsh Helleborine), W., D.
Ep. grandiflora (large white Hel.), W., D.
Ep. ensifolia (narrow leaved white Hel.), D.
Corallorhiza innata (spurless coral root), W.

JULY.

Orchis pyramidalis (pyramidal Or.), W., D.
Herminium monorchis (green musk Orchis), W., D.
Neottia spiralis (fragrant lady's tresses), D.
Epipactis latifolia (broad leaved Helleborine), Wo., D.
Ep. purpurata (purple leaved Hel.), Wo.
Malaxis paludosa (marsh bog Orchis), W.

JAMES EDWARDS,
Collector for Kew Gardens.

* W. Weald, Wo. Woods, D. Downs.

SOUTHDOWN BUTTERFLIES AND MOTHS.

There are a great many varieties of butterflies to be taken in Ditchling and the neighbourhood. Our British butterflies number over 60 specimens, 40 of which I have taken in the neighbourhood myself. They are as under :—

Argynnis Paphia	Silver washed Fritillary.
Argynnis Aglaia	Dark green Fritillary.
Argynnis Euphrosyne	Pearl-bordered Fritillary.
Argynnis Selene	Small pearl-bordered Fritillary.
Vanessa Urticæ	Small Tortoiseshell.
Vanessa Polychloros	Large Tortoiseshell.
*Vanessa Antiopa	Camberwell Beauty.
Io	Peacock.
Atalanta	Red Admiral.
Cardui	Painted Lady.
Melanagria Galathea	Marbled White.
Pyrarga Megæra	The Wall.
Satyrus Semele	Grayling.
Epinephele Janira	Meadow Brown.
Epinephele Tithonus	Large Heath.
Epinephele Hyperanthus	Ringlet.
Cænonympha Pamphilus	Small Heath.
Nemeobius Lucina	Duke of Burgundy.
Thecla Rubi	Green Hairstreak.
Thecla Quercus	Purple Hairstreak.
Polyommatus Phlæas	Common Copper.
Lycæna Icarus	Common Blue.
Lycæna Adonis	Clifden Blue.
Lycæna Corydon	Chalk-hill Blue.
Lycæna Alsus	Small Blue.
Lycæna Argiolus	Azure Blue.
Lycæna Medon	Brown Argus.
Colias Hyale	Pale Clouded Yellow.
Colias Edusa	Clouded Yellow.

* One taken in March, 1878.

Colias Helice	...	Variety of Clouded Yellow.
Rhodocera Ramni	...	Brimstone.
Anthocharia Cardamines	...	Orange-tip.
Pieris Napi	...	Green veined White.
Pieris Rapæ	...	Small White.
Brassicæ	...	Large White.
Hesperia Malvæ	...	Grizzled Skipper.
Hesperia Lavateræ	...	Scarce Grizzled Skipper.
Hesperia Tages	...	Dingy Skipper.
Hesperia Sylvanus	...	Large Skipper.
Hesperia Comma	...	Silver-spotted Skipper.
Hesperia Linea	...	Small Skipper.

Moths are also numerous, but time and space will not allow me to catalogue them. I may mention the Hawk-Moth, of which I have taken :—

Smerinthus ocellatus	...	Eyed Hawk-Moth.
Smerinthus populi	...	Poplar Hawk-Moth.
Smerinthus Tiliæ	...	Lime Hawk-Moth.
Acherontia Atropos	...	Death's-Head Hawk-Moth.
Sphinx Convolvuli	...	Convolvulus Hawk-Moth.
Sphinx Ligustri	...	Privet Hawk-Moth.
Chærocampa Porcellus	...	Small Elephant Hawk-Moth.
Chærocampa Elpenor	...	Elephant Hawk-Moth.
Macroglossa stellatarum	...	Humming Bird Hawk-Moth.
Macroglossa fuciformis	...	Broad-Bordered Bee Hawk-Moth.

NORMAN MERTON,
Ditchling.

CHATFIELD
Of Chailey, Westmeston, Chiltington and Ditchling.

(Compiled from original sources).

The earliest notices of the name of Chatfeld in Street Hundred are Theobald de Chattefeld who occurs in an Otehall deed about the 13th century. Walter Cattesfelde and Stephen Chatefield, of Westmeston, appear in the Poll Tax for 2 Rich. II. (1378). Walter C. occurs in a Wivelsfield deed in 1502. John C., Sen. and Jun., pay to the Subsidy of 14 and 15 Hen. VIII. in Street Hundred, also Thomas C., Sen. and Jun., and Richard and William. In 1536 Stevyn Chatfeld, of Saddlescombe, in Newtimber, makes his Will, and leaves 12d. to each of the High Altars of Newtimber and Hurst. He mentions his wife Alice and his sons Thomas, John, Stevyn, William and Edward, his daughters Agnes, Alice, Margaret and Eleanor. Thomas Luxford and Walter Dubbyll are the overseers of W. In the Sub. for Street Hundred, 37 Hen. VIII., Robert C. (? of Westmeston) is taxed "for the stock of Robert C. the son of Ro. C. for goods in his hands." In another Sub. for same date (1545) Robert C., of Westmeston, occurs, and also Richard C., of Chailey. In Sub. 5 Eliz., Robert C., Sen., appears under Lofeld, which was a township in south part of Chailey. In Subs. for 13 and 18 Eliz. for Street Hundred, Robert C. (? Chailey) and Nicholas and Robert C. (? of Chiltington with Westmeston) occur. In Subs. 43 Eliz. and 21 James, John C. of Chailey, John C. of Lofeld, Robert C. of Newick, and Robert C. of Ditchling, appear as landowners. Wills of these families from 1539 are at Probate Court, Lewes.

The pedigrees of "Chatfield of Bedyles in Ditchling" in the Herald's Visitations of Sussex, 1633 (Harl. and Add. MSS. in Brit. Mus.) and "Berry's Sussex Genealogies," are incorrect in stating that Thomas Chatfield and his son

John and grandson Richard were " of Bedyles," as this property did not come into the Chatfield family till 1614, when Thomas Haslegrove, of Ditchling, left by Will (pd. 1615) " his freehold lands in Ditchling " (Manor Rolls for D. give " Beadles ") " to his grandson Robert C. son of his only daughter and heir Margerie relict of John Cowper of Ditchling and afterwards wife of Robert Chatfield 'of Beards' in D." Thomas Chatfield, the head of the Visitation Pedigree, was perhaps of Chailey, and therefore tenant under the Lord of the Manor of Ditchling, in which the south part of that parish was. In Harl. MS. 1562, fo. 2, which is the Visitation of Sussex by Benolte in 1530, the Arms of Chatfeld are given, but no pedigree. Neither is there one in the original Visitation for 1574. Harl. MS., 892, and Add. MS. 6346 (which give the pedigree as from the original in 1574) are only transcripts with additions of late date and are in error.

PEDIGREE OF CHATFIELD.

Thomas Chatfield (? of Chayley, co. Sussex). Visitation = Alice, d. Richd. Stapley, of Twynham, co. Sussex (1633). of Sussex, 1633. Harl. MS. 1076, fo. 12ᵇ.

Children of Thomas Chatfield:

- **John C.** (? sen. of Chayley, subsidy 15 Hen. VIII, 1523. Vis. of Sussex, 1633.
- **Richard C.** = Agnes (1539), of Chailey (sub. 15 Hen. VIII, 1539.) Will 1539.
- **Roger C.**, dead before 1545. Sub. 37 Hen. VIII.
- **Robert C.**, (? of Westmeston), 37 Hen. VIII. Sub. Roll, 1545 (1539).
- **Thomas C.**, sen. (? of Chailey), 15 Hen. VIII, 1523. Sub. for Hund. of Street.
- **William C.**, 15 Hen. VIII, 1523. Sub. for H. of Street.

Next generation:

- **John C., jun.**, sub. Hund. of Street. 15 Hen. VIII. 1523.
- **Richard C.** = Elizabeth, d. John Brave, of Hove (? Widow D. Court Rolls 1602-7). (1633). of Chichester, Gent. Will 1586, at Chichester (1633).
- **Richard C.**, of Chailey (1539) Will 1552. mentions "Robert C., of Westmeston" Ob. S.P.
- **William C.**, of Chailey, W. 1560. S.P. (1552).
- **Robert C., sen.** = Joan (1589), of Hook in Chailey, Yeo. (1539). Sub. 5 Eliz. 1562. W. 1589-90.
- **Robert C., ? of Westmeston**, Sub. 37 Hen. VIII. 1545. Mentioned in Rich. C.'s Will 1552 as "Overseer."
- **Thomas C., of Chailey jun.**, 1523. W. 1558. = Agnes (1558).
- **John C., of** = **Sisely Chailey, Yeo. W. (1599). 1599-1600.**

Next generation:

- **Francis C., of Rumboldswick**, S. & H. W. P.C.C. 1594 (1633). = Ann, d. John Peckham (1633).
- **George C., Mayor of Chichester**, 1586. Died 1598. W. P.C.C.
- **Richard C., of Oving**, 1560 (Berry).
- Berry in error gives "Nicholas C., of Ditchling," 1. Jane, wife of Tho. Este. 2. Elizabeth, w. of Edwd. Monke. 3. Ann (1603)
- **Thomas C., ? of Ditchling.** W. 1603. Men. "Robt. C., Overseer." Bur. at D.
- **Ann** = **— Underhill, of Ditchling.** 1575
- **Robert C., of Chailey**, W. 1609.
- **John C., of Hook**, W. 1598. Sen. in 1598, D. Ct. Rolls.

Next generation:

- **Richard C.**, S. & H. = Cecilie Harrison (1633).
- Others.
- Francis C.
- George C.
- Thomas C.
- Jane C.
- Thomas C., bp. 1576.
- John C., bp. 1582.
- Richard C., bp. 1579. = — Gasgoyne.
- Richard C., bp. 1605 = 1664, Joan Jeffery.

- **Richard C.** =
- Richard C.

Henry C., bp. 1605; = 1664, Joan Jeffery.

and E. Chiltington. Sub. | (1610). | Sub. 13 Eliz., 1570, also
13 Eliz, 1570, also 1576. | 1575-1576. W. 1619.
W. 1610. Bur. at West-
meston.

- Richard C. of C'ton. W.1619. S.P.
- Edwd. C. (1619). Robt. C., of Lewes. W. 1628.
- Thos. C., of Chiltington, died 1653. W.
  - Nicholas C. Thos. C.
- Nicholas C. (1619).
  - John, Nicholas, Richd.

1. Richard C. 2. George C. 3. Robert C.,═1. 1596, Margery,
4. Thomas C. 5. Henry C.   of Beadles,   d. Thos. Hasle-
   1. Dennis, wife   1614, and of grove, of Beadles
      of — Worger.   Newick.   in D., and Relt.
                             W. 1629.   of John Cowper,
                                          of D.
                          ═2. 1600, Mary
                             Godley, of
                             Chayley.
                          ═3. Ann(1629)

Robert C., of D.,═? Unice
bp. 1597, d. 1660. (wid. 1662)
Bd. at Ditchling.   ob. 1663.

1. Robert C., of═   2. John C., of═Mary   3. William C.,═Sarah, d.
   Cuckfield, bp.   D., bp. 1632, Dwite, bp. 1639.   Michael
   1622, ob. 1680.   d. 1682 (1661)   1662 (D.   Marten.
   W.   Ct. Rolls.   Ct. Rolls.

                           2. John C., of═Susan   Robert C., of Street,═
                              1664,   Beckley. bp. 1677, d. 1736.
                              D.,

John C., of D.,═Mary   Robert C., bp. 1680. W.   Michael C., of═
bp. 1671, d.   Dwite,   Court Gardens
1754.   in D.
  Susan, wife   Robert C.,
  of John   of Street,
  Turner.

William C.,═Jane
bp.   bur.
d. 1689, of 1690.
Cardens
in D.

Robt. C.,   Jane,
D.S.P.   d. 1710.
1696.

Edmund C.,   John C.
bp.   (1629).
d. 1632.
W.
O.S.P.

Proofs of following Pedigree. Cheshire Add. MS. 5529, ff. 52^b, 53. Gloucestershire Harl. MSS. 1191, fo. 37^b; 1543, fo. 33. Inq. P.M. on Sir Gyles Poole. Will of Henry Poole 1580. Ditchling Parish Register. Monuments at Ditchling and Sapperton, &c.

Thomas Poole, of Poole, in Cheshire (sixth in descent from=Maud, dau. Thomas Sitton.
Robert Poole, of Poole, 21 Edw. I.), living 24 Henry VI.

1. Thomas Poole, of Poole, living 1 Edw. IV., died 1 Hen. VIII.

2. John Poole, servant to the=........
Lady Abbess of Wilton.

From whom descended in the 7th generation James Poole, of Poole, who was created a Baronet in 1677, and became the Ancestor of the Pooles of the Hook in County Sussex (vide Burke's Extinct Baronetage).

....Dau. of Danvers=2 Richard Poole, of Sapperton,=........dau. of Richard
(1st wife). | co. Gloucester, and Oaksey, co. | Souldwell, of Kent
            | Wilts. | (2nd wife).

1. Leonard=Catherine,   2. Henry Poole,=   3. William.   2 Daus.
Poole, of | dau. Sir   Ancestor of the
Sapperton,| Gyles   Wiltshire family
died 30th | Bridges,
Sep., 1539.| Kt.

2. Matthew Poole.
4. John Poole.

1. Sir Gyles Poole, Kt, of Sapperton,=   3. Henry Poole, of Ditchling Park, co. Sussex,=Margaret, dau.
died 28 Feb., 1588. In. P.M. (1580).   died 28 Mar., 1580. Will. Monument in Church. | George, Lord
                                                                                         Abergavenny.

Sir Henry Poole, Kt, of=   1. George.   3. Francis, of=Ann, dau. George Covert,   Katherine.   4. Thomas=Elizabeth,
Sapperton, born 1548, | 2. John.   Ditchling, | of Sutton Magna, co. Es- bur. 1558.   Poole, of | da. Roger
died 1616. Monument | 5. Henry.   1589. | sex, son of Richard Covert,   Lambeth, | Wingfield
in Church. | 6. William. | of Slaugham, co. Sussex,   died 1609.| of co.
                                                       | who died 1547.   Norfolk.

Walter Poole, bp. 1593.   1. Frances, bp. 1576.   Charles   Thomas,   ? 2 Daus.
                           2. Margaret, bp. 1591, bd. 1591.   (1580).   bp. 1591.

*PEDIGREE OF ATTREE OF WIVELSFIELD.

(1.)

John Atte Ree, Lord of the === Joan, dau. and co-heir of Walter
Manor of Otehall, 1438.   Atte Hurst, alias Walter Othale.

John At Ree, of Wivelsfield, a Collector of a Subsidy for Sussex, 1488, Lord of Otehall.

William Atte Ree or A"Tree, Lord of Otehall in 1502 === Agnes, d. and h. of Thomas === John Atte Ree of === ......
and 1504. With his wife, Agnes, sold lands in   Freshfield, in Wiv-   Wivelsfield, Sen.
Horsted Keynes in 1497.   elsfield. Died   De Banco Rolls.
                                                 A. in 1481.

                                                                                      John Atte Ree,
                                                                                      of Wivelsfield,
                                                                                      Junr.

Thomas Atte Ree or Attree, === ......   John AtRee, of === ......   Richard Atte Ree, of === ......   Richard Attree, of Theo- === before 1527,
Lord of Otehall, 1523-1537.   Lockstrood, in   'Theobalds, in Wiv-   balds and Webbs in   Joan,
                                           Wivelsfield.   elsfield. Died 1527.   Wivelsfield. Died 1544. d. . . . Sherry.
                                           Died 1559. W.   W.

Dau. and Heir === Walter Godman.

See Ped. in Sussex Arch.
Coll., Vol. xxxv.

Roger AtRee, === ......
of Horsted
Keynes.

Thomas Att Ree, === ......   John Attree === Eleanor.   Joan.   Jane. Eleanor. Agnes.
of Town Place, in   of   m.   m.
Horsted Keynes.   Lockstrood.   Chrisr.   Edw.
Died 1533.   John Attree === Elizabeth, d.   Mit-   Lee.
                                                            Born 1534.   Edmund Mit-   chell,
                                                            Died 1583.   chell, of Cuck-   of Cuck-
                                                            W.   field, W. 1603.   Turke-
                                                                                                field.
Richard, a minor   John Attree, of   1558.
in 1533. Died   Town Place,   John Attree, === Elizabeth, d.
1546.   1546. For issue
                   see Ped. 2.   See Ped. in S.A.C., Vol. xxxv.

* Proofs from Otehall Deeds, De Banco Rolls, Horsted Keynes Court Rolls, Wills and Parish Registers.

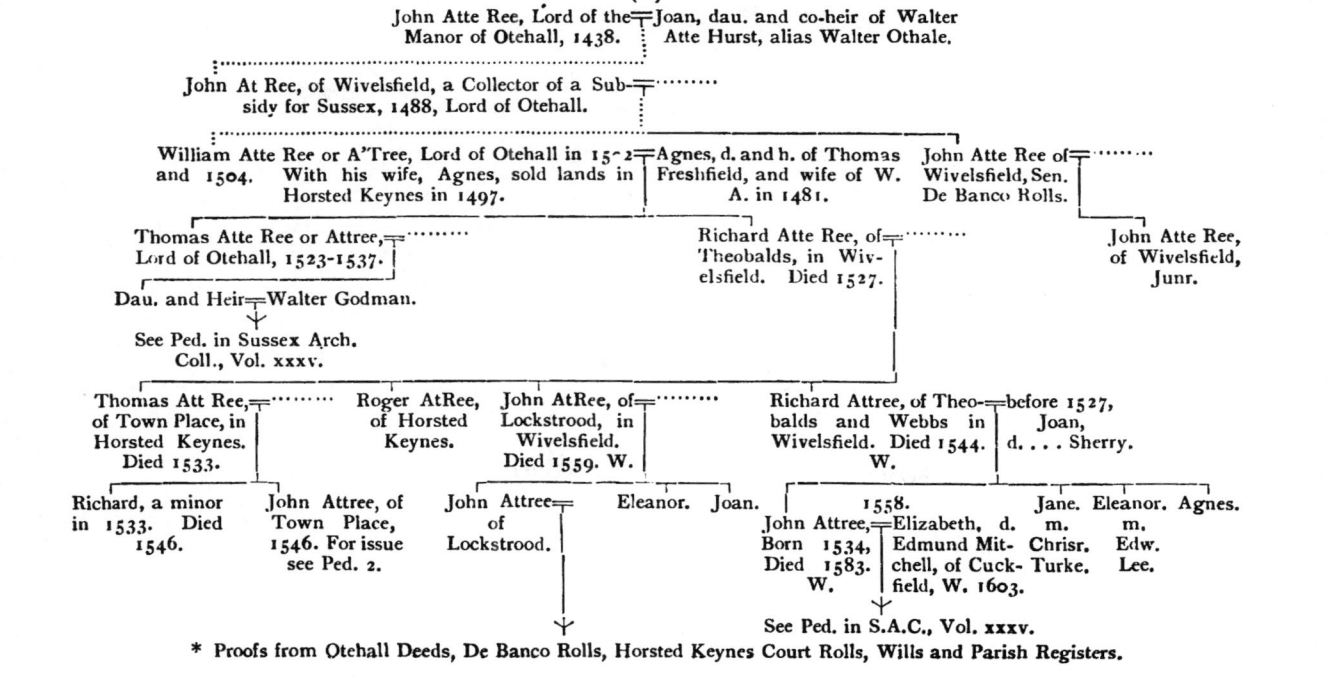

*PEDIGREE OF ATTREE OF BARCOMBE AND DITCHLING.

(2.)

John Attree, of Barcombe, Co. Sussex, = 1563, Margaret, wid. of Richard Trenborn about 1530, died 1610, W. in dell, of Hurstpierpoint, buried at Barcombe 1606.
P.C.C. He is presumed to be the 2nd son of Thomas Atte Ree of Town Place, in Horsted Keynes, who died 1533. (See Ped. 1).

James A., b. 1567, d. 1606.

Richard A., of Rother-=Alice Barnfield, d. 1629, W., den.
P.C.C., was fined for Knighthood, but died before the fine was collected in 1631.

William Attree, of Rodmel, d., s. p.

Thomas A., of=1608, Joan, Wivelsfield, b. 1576, d. 1641. W. | dau. John Attree, of Lockstrood.

Jane Attree, b. 1573, m. 1592 Henry Heaseman, of Barcombe.

William Attree, of Ditchling, who d. 1659, and left issue Jessie Attree, of Street, and Thomas A., of Ditchling.

John A., d. 1585.

John A., of Brighton, who married and left an only dau.

John Joan

William Attree, of Barcombe, bap. at Barcombe,=1. 1607, Anna Patcham.
1583, d. and bur. at Barcombe, 1654. W., P.C.C. | 2. 1642, Jane Alford.

Anna, b. 1608, m. 1632, | John A.,=1631, | William Attree, | Thos. A. | Edward A.,=1. Ann Peckham,
Ric. Coppard, of Newick. | b. 1609, Judith | of Fletching, b. | b. 1618, | of Bar- | d. 1649.
2. Mary, b. 1611, m. 1631, | d. 1653, Oliffe. | 1613, d. 1683, | d. 1625. | combe, | 2. Mary Prior.
1. Ric. Howell, 2. Ric. | W. | W. Lewes. | | b. 1621,
Acton. | P.C.C. | | | d. 1684.

		tree, Woodman, b. 1650, d. 1721. d. 1690, of Fletching. W. Lewes.

...... , ..., ...
William, b. 1645, m. 1671, John Devall.
Mary, b. 1646, d. 1648.
Jane, b. 1648, m. 1674, John Stocker.
Ann, b. 1648, m. 1674, John Stocker.
Jane, m. Rob. Bennett.
Edward, b. 1656.
Elizabeth, b. 1658.
Edward, b. 1660, and d. 1725, m. and left issue.
Thomas, b. 1661.

John Attree, of ——— ..., u. 10/9, Mary Russell
Fletching, bap. (= 2. 1686 Saml.
there in 1652, Awcock), d. 1718.
d. 1684. Adm. Adm.
Lewes.

William Attree, of Ditch— | 1707, Elizabeth   Ann A., m.
ling, bp. at Fletching, | Jarrett, b. 1682, 1706, Will.
1681, d. and bur. at | d. 1741.   Smith.
Ditchling 1747. W.

Elizabeth A., b. 1713,
m. 1744, John Fuller,
of More House, Wiv-
elsfield.

Jane, d. John ═══ 1745, Susan Scrase
Attree, d. 1743. (and wife).
Bp. at D. 1708, d. 1772, W.

John,   Jane,
B. 1741. B. 1742.
B. 1742. B. 1744.

John Attree, of Ditchling,   William Attree, of   Harry Attree, of   Richard Attree, of   Sukey, mar.
b. 1747, d. 1801, W. He   Brighton, b. 1749,   Brighton and   Isfield, b. 1757, d. 1. John Saxby.
mar. 1st—1773, Dorothy   d. 1810, W. He   Ditchling, b. 1752, 1842. He mar.   2. John Bull.
Mill, who d. 1784, and 2nd mar. 1773, Frances   d. 1835, mar.   Mary Rogers, and
—Sarah Frances Turner,   Blackman, of   Anne Robinson,   left issue.
of Oldland, by whom he   Southover, and left   and left issue.
left issue. Vide S.A.C.,   issue. Vide Burke's
Vol. xxv., Pedigree of   "Family Records"
Turner of Oldland.   and Howard's
                            "Visitation of Eng-
                            land and Wales."

Mary,   Sukey, mar.
Susan,   1. John Saxby.
d. infants. 2. John Bull.

* Proofs from Otehall Deeds, De Banco Rolls, Horsted Keynes Court Rolls, Wills and Parish Registers.

INDEX.

Abergavenny Chapel, 59.
Abergavenny, George Neville, Lord, 13.
Abergavenny, Marquis of, 21.
Acton, Henry, 119.
Adeane, Richard, ext. from will, 9.
Administrators, Ditchling, 149, 150.
Agate family, 107, 114; memorial, 107; Stephen, 113, 114; Thomas, 116, 117, 128.
Alfred the Great, 2, 3, 5, 35, 36, 57.
Alicia, wife of John de Warenne, 14.
Amicia, wife of William Hocote, 18.
Anderida, forest of, 2.
Arundel, Countess of, 21; Earls of, 6, 21.
Ash, Rev. John George and family, 87.
Ashburnham, Denny (Vicar), 77, 86, 87.
Ashburnham family, 87.
Assault, cases of, 17, 18.
Atte Ree, John, 100.
At Ree, Richard, 73, 100; William, 100.
Attree, Edmund, 76; family, 73, 100, 105; memorials, 100-102, 105; Thomas, 52. 87, 101.
Ayleboyne, Richard (Vicar), 76.

Backman, Thos., 113
Bacun, John, 18.
Bailey, Joseph (Vicar), 77, 86.
Baptists, early, 114.
Beard, Thos., 83.
Beatrix, Countess of Arundel, 22.
Bell, Theobold de la (Rector), 76.
Bennett, Abraham, 117.
Bergavenny, Lords, 21, 22.

Billinghurst family, 116, 117; memorials, 117.
Bland, Edward, 74.
Boadle, Mrs., 128.
Boarman, John, 114.
Boddington memorials, 109; Trust, 75.
Borde family, 13.
Borrer memorials, 109.
Bridgeman, Thomas (Vicar), 77, 78.
Brighthelmstone Races, 125; diversions at, 125.
Brighton Chain Pier (anecdote), 50, 51.
Brompton, William (Rector), 76, 78.
Browne Burial Yard, 120, 121; family, 35, 114, 119; James, 114, 119, 120; Peter, 114, 121; William, 119.
Browne, Francis, 81.
Buckley, John (Vicar), 77, 82.
Bull Bait, a, 125.
Bull, Charles, 107.
Bull memorials, 107
Bull Inn, 48, 51.
Burgess, John, 116; "Jernel,' 122-130.
Burne, John de, 20.
Burnell, Nicholas (Rector), 76, 78.
Burrell MSS, 9, 75.
Butterflies and Moths, 155, 156.

Caffin, John and Bridget, memorial, 114.
Caffyn, Matthew, 110, 114
Camois Court Manor, 6, 12.
Campion, Rev. William, 118.
Centenarians, 92, 108.

INDEX.

Chaloner family, 105, 106, 137.
Chapel, ancient record of a, 71, 72.
Chapel Church, 130; House, 137.
Chapel (dissenting), 110-121, anniversary, 121; early members, 114; families connected with, 119; founder of, 113.
Chapel Royal, Brighton, 86.
Chapman, John (Vicar), 76.
Chatfield family, 46, 94, 107, 113, 122, 128, 129, 137, 157, 158; of Bedyles, 46; John, 107; John and Robert, 118; John and Susan, 113; Michael, 46; Michael of Court Gardens, 113, 128; of Oving, 46; Robert, senr. and junr., 113; Robert, of Street, 113; Sarah, 127, 128.
Chattefeld, Theobold, de, 46.
Chatfield, memorial, 107, 129.
Charities and Trusts, 74, 75.
Chester, Bishop of, 19.
Chesterfield, Earl of, 45.
Chichester, Chancellor of, 9, 78; Dean and Chapter, 9.
Chiltington, 136, 137.
Chitterne, John de (Rector), 76, 78.
Church Bells and Plate, 65.
Churchwardens' accounts, 75, 80; list of, 151, 153.
Clarke, William, 78.
Clayton Church frescoes, 138.
Cleres, Chase of, 22.
Clers, Foresters of, 17.
Cleves, Lady Anne of, 11, 12, 28, 31-34, 72, 78.
Cliffe Church clock, 129.
Coaching period anecdotes, 48, 49.
Coke, John (Vicar), 76.
Couplet, an old, 66.
Court Gardens, 113, 122, 128.
Cripps, John Martin, 106.
Cromwell, Lord, 11.
Croseby, Richard (Vicar), 76.
Crump, John (Vicar), 77, 83.
Cuckfield, 139.
Culpepper family, 90.

Dancy family, 84, 114; John, 114;
Josiah, 116; Mary, 114; memorials, 114; Thomas and Mary, 83.
Dann, Richard, 109.
Danny Park, 138.
Dansey, James, 54.
Davies, Mr., 117.
Denton, Edward (Vicar), 77, 78; family, 78.
Deudeney memorial, 94.
Devil's Dyke, 2, 139
Dicul, Abbot of Bosham, 3.
Dimocks Manor, 6, 9, 11, 12.

DITCHLING.
 Administrators, 149, 150.
 Alexander de, 11.
 Beacon, 1, 131, 133, 134, 135.
 Borstal, 48, 133.
 "Busy end" of, 47.
 Common, 1, 9, 39, 41.
 Churchwardens, 151, 153.
 Downs, 9.
 Garden Manor, 6, 9-12
 Gooseberries, 52, 53.
 Horticultural Society, 52.
 Manor of, 2, 3, 6, 21, 22.
 Origin and various forms of the word, 2, 3.
 Park, 3, 6, 14, 17, 18, 22, 25-27, 33, 34.
 Prosecution Society, 51, 52.
 Rectors of, 76.
 Rectory of, 71.
 Rectory Manor or Dimocks, 6, 9, 11, 12.
 Subsidy Rolls, 140-145.
 Vicarage, 50, 76.
 Vicars of, 76-77.
 Wills, 146-149.
Dobel, Daniel, 114.
Dobel family, 137.
Domesday extracts, 4, 5.
Dorrell Trust, 75.
Doust, Edward, 114.
Downs, South, 1, 34, 119, 133, 135.
Drowley, James, 116, 128.
Duncton Down, 133.
Duplock, Gideon, 119.

INDEX.

Dwite, Ann, memorial, 108; will, 108.
Dychenynge, John de, 20.

Edward the Confessor, 4, 5.
,, I., 18, 20.
,, II., 20, 54.
,, III. and Queen, corbel-heads of, 58.
,, Prince at Lewes, 14-16.
,, First Prince of Wales, 18-20.
Elizabeth, Princess, 34; Queen, 9, 138.
Esdaile, Mr., 119.
Ethelwulf, 2.
Evershed, William, 114, 115, 128.
Evesham, Battle of, 17.

Fairs, 39, 40, 41, 48, 54.
Falmer, Alfrey de, 11.
Ferriss, John (Vicar), 76.
Ferryng, John de, 18.
Feudal Rights, exercise of, 17-18.
Feyrher, Richard (Vicar), 76.
Field, Thomas, 65.
Fitz-Alan family, 6, 21.
Fletching Common, Barons at, 15.
Foster, Richard, 114.
Foresters of Clers, 17; De Warenne, 18; Waldon, 17.
Frankbarrough, 22.
Frescoes at Clayton, 138; Westmeston, formerly at, 137.
Fritebergh and Shortfrith, 22.
Fuller memorial, 109.
Funderhay, Robert (Vicar), 76.
Funeral, mistake at a, 88-89.

Gaveston, Piers, 18-20.
Geymyshe, John (Vicar), 76.
Gilbert, Mr., 121.
Giles, Mascall (Vicar), 77, 81, 82; family, 81.
Glebe Lands, 9.
Godman, Walter, 100.
Gott family, 137.
Gravett, John (Vicar), 77, 82.
Grimes, Thomas, 121.

Gundrada, Countess, 4, 10.
Gurnell, Thomas (Vicar), 76.

Haldeleye, Walter de, 17.
Hamper, William (notes on Ditchling), 61.
Hanley, John (Vicar), 77, 86.
Harold, King, 4.
Harraden, Edward, 65.
Harris, Jacob, 41-43.
Harris, Thomas (Clerk), 76.
Hastings, Battle of, 4.
Hastings, Matthew de, 17.
Hause, Constance, memorial, 93; Will, 93.
Hawes family, 94.
Henry III., 14-16.
Henry VIII., 11, 28, 33, 71, 72.
Hether, Joane, dau. of Richard, 73.
Hider, Henry, 78.
Hider, Richard, 114.
Higginbotham, Sarah, 81.
Higgons, Humfry (Vicar), 76, 78.
Holbein, 28.
Holinshed, 33.
Hollingbury copse, 31.
Hoptide or Hocktide, 6.
Horsham, assizes at, 43, 127.
Hougham memorial, 90.
Howard, Katherine, 33.
Howell, George (centenarian), 108, 109
Hudson, Thomas (Vicar), 77, 86.
Hurstpierpoint Church, 138.
Hussey's notes on Church, 60.
Hutchinson, Thomas (Vicar), 61, 65, 77, 88.

Iver, Elnathan (Vicar), 39, 40, 77, 84; memorial, 84.

Jackson, Rev., 129, 130.
Jacob's Post, 43.
James, Henry, tragic death of, 87.
Jefferies, Samuel (Vicar), 77, 85; memorial, 85, 86.
Jointure, 122.

Kempe, Sergeant, 12, 13.

INDEX.

Kennaday, James, 119.
Keymer, 138.
Kite, Mr., 119.

Lamb, William (Vicar), 77, 84; family, 85.
Lane family, 12.
Lanzo, Prior, 10.
Lewes, 3, 16; Battle of, 15-16, 135; Lords of, 14; Mise of, 16.
Lewrey, Daniel and Rose, 114.
Leopard, George, 114.
Linch Down, 133.
Lindfield, 139.
Linfield, Edward (Vicar), 76, 78.
Lloyd, Dr. Charles, 117.
Lodge Farm, 25; Hill, 27.
London, a journey to, 126.
Longevity of inhabitants, 108.
Looker family, 128; James, 129.
Love Feast and washing of feet, 115.
Lucas Charity, 75; family, 13.
Lulham, Edward (Vicar), 77, 82; family, 82.

Macdougal, Alexander, 121.
Manors of Ditchling, 2, 3, 6, 13, 21, 22, 59; Ditchling Rectory, 6, 9, 11, 12, Ditchling Garden, 6, 9-12; Camois Court, 6, 12; Pellingworth, 6, 12, 13.
Mansion, discovery of foundations, 25.
Mantell, Gideon Algernon, 120.
Marchant, diary, extracts from, 39, 40.
Marchant family, 93; Nicholas, 83; Peter, memorial and will, 93.
Margaret, St., of Antioch, 54.
Markets and Fairs, 20-21, 47-48.
Marten family, 106, 114; Michael, 106, 108, 113, 114; of "Furl," 116; Peter, funeral, 128.
Mascall, John, 81; Leonard, 136.
Mattock, Anthony (Vicar), 77, 79; John and William, 79.
Meeting House, 110-121.
Medley, Thomas, 13.
Michael, Sampson (Vicar), 76.

Michelbourne, alias Mascall, 73; family, 72-74, 90, 94; John, 73; Sir Richard, 73; Richard, senr. and junr., 73; Thomas, 73.
Miles, Richard and Dorothy, 41-42.
Mise of Lewes, 16.
Mitford, Richard, Bp. of Chichester, 72.
Moir, Mr., 121.
Molly, Aunt, 119-121.
Montfort. Simon de, 15, 135.
More, John, of Morehouse, 9.
Morgan, Rev., 46, 110, 130.
Morgan, William, 12.
Morrell, Dr., 119.
Mortaine, Earl of, 4, 5.
Mott, Isaac, 116; Sally, 127.

Neville family, 6, 21-22; Edward Lord Bergavenny, 22; George Lord Abergavenny, 13; Sir Henry, 22.
Newington, Edmund de (Rector), 76.
Newtimber, 138.
Nicholls, John (Vicar), 77, 83, 84; family, 84.
Niwent, John de, 17.
Norton, Francis Collins (Vicar), 77, 89.
Nouaille, Julius (Vicar), 77, 87; memorial, 88.

Oldland, 40, 72, 73, 138.
Orchis, list of, 154.
Osferth, 3, 4.
Otehall. 138.
Overy, William George, Francis and Robert, 22.
Owls, white, 67-68.
Ox, a remarkable, 126.
Ox Teams, 134.

Park Farm, 25, 27; Barn, Corner, 27.
Parker, John (Vicar), 77, 83.
Parker, Walter, 17.
Patrons of Living, 71, 78.
Peckham, Edward (Vicar), 76, 78; family, 78.
Pellingworth Manor, 6, 12, 13.

INDEX.

Phillips, J. O. Halliwell, 31.
Place House, 35, 120.
Plumpton Church, 136; Cross (incised), 135, 136; Hugh de, 11; Place, 135, 136; Plain, 16, 135.
Poachers, prosecution of, 21.
Pocoke, Richard, visit to Ditchling, 45.
Pokehole, 17.
Poole, family of, 98; Henry, 34, 97; Margaret, 97, 98; Monument, 34, 97; extract from Will, 98, 99.
Porter, Rev. Mr., of Chailey, 40.
Powell, Edward (Vicar), 77, 85; Jane, 85; memorial, 85, 99.
Poynings Church, 138, 139.
Preston Manor House, 31.
Price, Thomas (Vicar), 77, 81; family, 81.
Price, Mrs., 79-81.
Price, Sarah, memorial, 94.
Pritchett, Thomas, 81.
Pye, Henry (Vicar), 77, 78.
Pyecombe, 138.

Quarrel, an amusing, 79, 80.
Queen's Park, Brighton, 101, 102.

Rawood, Hugh (Vicar), 77, 79; family, 79, 81; Anne Warren, 80; Mrs., 79-81.
Rectors, list of, 76.
Registers, early names in, 75; extracts from, 78, 79, 81-85, 87, 93.
Reygate, John de, 18.
Rhyme, extract from local, 43.
Roman Remains, 1, 2.
Richard, King of Romans, 14, 15.
Richards, Edward (Vicar), 77.
Richmond, Palace of, 31, 34.
Rideout, Rev., 130.
Robbery at Brown's and sequel, 126, 127.
Rookery, 122, 125.
Rose, John (Clerk), 76.
Rottingdean, Phillip de, 11.
Rowes MS., extract from, 22.
Royal Oak Inn, Tragedy at, 41, 42.
Russell, Dr., 12.
Rygge, William, 10.

Rysshton, John (Vicar), 76.

St. Margaret's Church, 54-68; Feast of, 20; Head of, 59; Legend of, 54.
St. Pancras, Prior of, 9, 10, 72; Priory of, 10-12, 14, 71, 78.
St. Wilfrid, 3.
Sade, Alexander, 11.
Sadler, Thomas, 117.
Sale, John (Vicar), 76.
Sampson, Dr. Cooper, 44.
Saxby, John, memorial, 106.
Saxon skeleton, discovery of, 57.
Schools, Lancastrian, 118, 119.
"Scool," Sunday, 127.
Scrase family, 106.
Seagrave, Lord, 15.
Seffrid II., Bp. of Chichester, 71.
Seymour, Jane, 28.
Shelley, Henry, J.P., 82.
Shortfrith, 22.
Shyre, Alexander de, 18
Simmonds, Brother John, 116.
Singers, Ditchling, 66, 67.
Smith family, 12, 13.
Smith family memorials, 108; "Jon," 116.
Smythe, 73.
Snell, Samuel (Vicar), 77, 82; family, 82.
Snellgrove, Mr., 117.
South Downs, 1, 34, 119, 133, 135; Sheep, 134; Shepherd, 134.
South Down Butterflies and Moths, 155, 156.
Springett, Rev. Anthony, 118.
Sprot, Isabel, 74.
Sprotts' Charity, 74.
Squier, John Owen, 119.
Standean, Lower, Corn tithes of, 74.
Stanford, Rebecca, 78.
Stanmer, 13, 135.
Stantons, 106, 108, 114, 137.
Stapley, Anthony, 12.
Stevens, William, 119.
Streat Church and Place, 137.
Subsidy Rolls, 140-145.
Surrey, Earls of, 14, 21.

INDEX.

Tanner family, 106.
Theobalds, 73, 76.
Thompson, Samuel, memorial, 114.
Tiles, discovery of ancient, 26.
Tinwood, Mr., 121.
Tithes, Rectorial, 72, 73.
Todeherst, John, 11.
Tragedy at Royal Oak, 41-42.
Trusts, 75.
Tuppen, family memorials, 99-100.
Turke, Agnes, dau. of Christopher and Joan, 73.
Turner, family of, 73, 90-93; John, 73; Richard, 39; Thomas, 73; memorials, 90-93; at Keymer, 138.
Turner, Rev., 130.
Turner, Robert and Alfred, 121.

Valor Ecclesiasticus, extracts, 9, 10.
Vicars, list of, 76-77.
Vincent, John (Rector), 76.

Walder, James, 116.
Waldon, Foresters of, 17.
Walter, Daniel (Vicar), 77, 85.
Warenne, Earls de, 6, 10, 11; family, 10, 14, 71; John de, 14-18; John, eighth Earl, 20, 21; William de, 4; William, second Earl, grant by, 10.
Watson, Anthony, Bp. of Chichester, 74, 79.
Water mill (Domesday), 4, 5.
Webb family, 108.
Westmeston Church, 137; Jubilee Memorial, 137.
Westwick, 6.
Wheatears, 134, 135.
White, Nicholas, 82.
Whitgift, Archbishop, 74.
William the Conqueror, 4, 14.
Williams, Thomas, 78.
Wills, list of Ditchling, 146-149.
Willys, William (Vicar), 77, 83; family, 83.
Wings Place, 35, 36; Croft (note), 35.
Wissett, Sir Oliver de, 20.
Withall, Rev. Geo., 119.
Wivelsfield, 9, 71, 78, 138.
Wode, Ralph (Vicar), 76.
Wood, James, 65, 94; family, 94; Thomas, 113.
Woollen, burials in, 83, 84.
Worth, Forest of, 22.